When You Say "Thank You," *Mean It*

... And 11 Other Lessons for Instilling Lifelong Values in Your Children

When You Say "Thank You," Mean It

Mean It

... *And 11 Other Lessons for Instilling Lifelong Values in Your Children*

Mary O'Donohue

Foreword by Nancy Lilienthal, MS Ed

Avon, Massachusetts

Published by Adams Media, a division of F+W Media, Inc.
57 Littlefield Street, Avon, MA 02322. U.S.A.
www.adamsmedia.com

ISBN 10: 1-4405-0377-X
ISBN 13: 978-1-4405-0377-1
eISBN 10: 1-4405-0874-7
eISBN 13: 978-1-4405-0874-5

Printed in the United States of America.

10 9 8 7 6 5 4 3 2 1

Library of Congress Cataloging-in-Publication Data
is available from the publisher.

This publication is designed to provide accurate and authoritative
information with regard to the subject matter covered. It is sold with
the understanding that the publisher is not engaged in rendering legal,
accounting, or other professional advice. If legal advice or other expert
assistance is required, the services of a competent professional person
should be sought.

—From a *Declaration of Principles* jointly adopted by a
Committee of the American Bar Association and
a Committee of Publishers and Associations

Many of the designations used by manufacturers and sellers to distinguish
their product are claimed as trademarks. Where those designations appear
in this book and Adams Media was aware of a trademark claim, the designations have been printed with initial capital letters.

This book is available at quantity discounts for bulk purchases.
For information, please call 1-800-289-0963.

dedication

To Jim, Connor, and Grace,
with infinite gratitude

"*Live your beliefs and you can turn the world around.*"

~Henry David Thoreau

contents

foreword

As the director of a preschool in Manhattan, and an educator with thirty years of experience, it has been a continual source of joy to me throughout my professional career to watch young children start to explore the world around them. In the rapid development of these first few years, everything is new and exciting for them as they learn to interact with their world and their fellow human beings. As a parent, I have also experienced first-hand the pleasures and challenges of helping my own daughter and son grow to become caring, responsible adults who make me proud every day.

That's every parent's wish. But many parents don't realize that morals are not something that spring naturally from human beings. In other words, children will not simply absorb your moral character if you don't take the time to talk with them and teach them right from wrong.

Jean Piaget, the Swiss psychologist who devoted his career to the study of children and how they learn, would tell you that children are not born with values. An infant's entire focus is on the need to survive. If they are hungry, their energy goes to letting someone know and getting fed. Their brains are not capable of taking in the needs of others. Around the age of two or three, however, that begins to change and the world around them becomes very interesting. With this interest come challenges that are new to the child. New questions arise, such as "How do I get what I want but also make my friend or parent happy?" Sometimes young children will revert to those egocentric ways, but more and more what is happening around them becomes important to them. This is the moment for parents or other adults who share their lives to start to guide. Certainly, setting an example for the child is essential, both by how the adult treats the children and others around them. From my experience, I know that adults must show respect not only to the child, but also to those around them. A teacher who shows great respect to the children but is disrespectful to co-teachers does not set a good example—and children are very perceptive.

You show respect to children when you let them know you care about them, and care about what they think and how they feel. But beginning this process of learning values with young children also requires additional help from adults. Sometimes children cannot find the words they need to tell their peers how they feel. Here an adult can step in and *help* (without taking over) the children to discover a way to work it out that is considerate of everyone.

But what about older children who have the abilities but still need help? Setting examples is a great start, but it is not enough. Just as children learn about history and science, they need to learn about values. They must be challenged to think about the whys, hows, whens, and wheres of values. When younger, they thought about how to get what they wanted and how to please others; now they have to learn to think of more abstract ideas, such as, "What does it mean to me and others when I show compassion?" "What is important to me?" "How should I behave toward others?" We do not want children to follow values solely because adults tell them to, but because these values are part of who they are.

In this book, Mary O'Donohue has set out a process for helping your family take an in-depth look at the important values in your own life. This process has given Mary and her husband the chance to focus attention on what is important to them and why, and she has found a way for other families to do the same. Mary and her husband started their children on this program when each of them was five, which is the youngest age children can truly learn from these exercises. Mary has provided many variations in her monthly exercises so that any family can focus on the values that are most important to them in a way that works for them. She provides the blueprint to know how to break down those values so that children will truly understand them. The more involved the children are, not only in the exercises but also in the planning, the more they will be able to internalize the values.

There are opportunities everywhere that provide openings for a conversation with your child about values. Take every moment you can to talk to your child about how you feel about things. Challenge them to reach down within themselves and talk about how they feel and, if action needs to happen, how they can go about doing that.

When my children were young and growing up in New York City, many homeless people lived on the streets in our neighborhood. Instead of rushing past without taking notice, we often talked about how these people had become homeless and how we could help. We could not give money to everyone who asked, but we could collect coats and clothing that we could give to organizations that could help them. We also talked about how they still deserved our respect even if their lives were very different. Taking the time in our day to talk about it made the issue important.

In our overcrowded world, people are constantly interacting with each other. With the Internet, even people who are isolated physically can still be in constant contact with others. How are we all going to get along? Maybe we can all help a little by taking the time to pass on to our children those values that have made us better people, better citizens, and better members of the human race.

Nancy Lilienthal, MS Ed,
Director of 43rd Street Kids Preschool

introduction

As a parent, I'm sure you've had a moment (or two) when you wonder if you're teaching your children values in a way that's actually getting through to them. I know I have. The one that sticks with me most was when my son Connor was about five years old and he received a gift from a friend of mine. She had found a blue-patterned T-shirt she thought he would like, and presented it to him wrapped in cheerful paper with a colorful ribbon. When my son tore open the gift and saw the T-shirt, he was clearly disappointed. Apparently, he had hoped it might be a toy or game. Connor carelessly dropped the shirt on the floor and started to walk out of the room, stepping over strips of wrapping paper as he went. I remember saying the all too familiar "Hey . . . what do you say?" and he had replied with a lackluster, *"Thaaank youuuu"* with barely a glance in our direction. Not much of a proud moment for me, but probably a familiar one for many parents.

I was embarrassed and disappointed. Not just in my son, but in my husband and myself as well. I also felt a bit defensive and guilty. My husband and I were certainly both busy parents, working inside the home, outside the home, and to and from the home. At least that's what it felt like sometimes. And our son's childhood was moving along all too quickly. We are not experts on values, nor do we claim to live our values perfectly. But we were *genuinely* trying to teach our son our values. We were striving to do our best every day—not only for us, but also because we were committed to providing a good example for our son. Somehow that had not proven to be enough.

And we valued gratitude. Hadn't we modeled polite behavior all the time? Hadn't we taught our son to say "thank you" each and every time someone gave him a gift?

It bothered me for days before I had an epiphany. We'd never actually taught our son to be thankful. Not once. All we had ever done was to *train* him to *act* thankful. In terms of true gratitude, we hadn't even scratched the surface. Even if he had actually spoken the words "thank you" to my friend that day, how would it have mattered if he hadn't been feeling the accompanying gratitude? And clearly he hadn't been. What if she had given him a toy? Something he actually wanted. I imagine he would have jumped up and down and gleefully exclaimed "thank you, thank you!" But even that would probably not have been gratitude. Happiness, sure, but not gratitude.

After giving it a great deal of thought, I came up with an idea to celebrate "Gratitude Month." We spent an entire month focusing on teaching our son about being grateful. We made a gratitude poster illustrating things he was thankful for. We talked about how important it was to be grateful for all the blessings we had in our lives. We taped pictures and sayings about gratitude on the walls of the playroom. In short, we made gratitude the focus of our month. And I remember telling my son to think about *why* he was thankful every time he said "thank you" so it wouldn't be just about the words, it would really be about the feeling behind the words. Over the course of that month, we saw a change Connor. He had started to become a truly grateful person. At the time, we felt like the gratitude lesson had been accomplished and didn't realize that this was the beginning of something even more significant in our lives. A few months later, our daughter Grace joined the family, and life seemed to move faster than ever.

The years flew by and one day when Grace was five and Connor was ten, I caught my daughter trying to shoplift at a local store. She had tried stuffing a candy bar in her pocket, and then lied about it when I caught her and insisted she put it back. It certainly wasn't grand theft or anything, but it was a wake-up call for me as a parent. I was forced to admit that even though my husband and I were trying to live as kind, compassionate, honest people, we weren't consciously *teaching* our values to our children, not in the way that gets below the surface and sticks. We were living our values, and modeling them and talking about them on a regular basis. But it wasn't enough. Our children were getting older and I began to wonder if we were doing a good job of teaching them what truly mattered to us. Did they even know what our values were?

So one spring evening shortly after that, my husband and I sat down with our children and I asked, "What is important to me and Daddy? Do you know?" They looked stumped for a moment and then both replied, almost in unison, "We are. We're really important to you." Of course, nothing is more important to us than our children, but that wasn't what I was trying to get at. I wanted to know if they knew what our *values* were, so I mentioned that I was looking for something like kindness. My daughter said "Kindness, mom. That's important to you." Needless to say, it wasn't going too well at this point. Then my son offered "Gratitude. I know you always believe in being thankful." "That's great!" I said. "Anything else?" Neither of them could come up with another thing.

After that conversation, I knew we had to make a change. The one thing that gave me hope was that Connor had brought up gratitude. It struck me that if a lesson like that had stayed with him for five years, maybe we had really been on to something. We couldn't go on teaching values in the kind of haphazard way we had been doing for the last few years. We had to have a plan, and we had to stick with it.

I sat down with a pen and paper and wrote down, "What Really Matters to Us." I talked with my husband and within a week or so, we had a list of the values that have been a road map for our lives. When I looked at the final list, I counted twelve core values. *Hmm.* Twelve months in a year. I knew I had found my direction. Over the course of the next few weeks, I started to create basic exercises for each value, and within a month, my family and I embarked on a new and improved Gratitude Month to start off our yearlong journey of focusing on values. I continued to develop and refine the exercises for each value (with lots of feedback from my kids) as we experienced each new month. Over time, I had a system for teaching values to my children.

This program is based on values my husband and I share, but the book is designed so that you can do these exercises, or use them as inspiration to create exercises of your own. The twelve values in this book are the ones that matter most to my husband and me, but they may not be *your* top twelve values. Sure, maybe we have some in common—maybe even most of them. But what if you feel strongly that leadership, cooperation, or loyalty are values you want your children to have? No worries—this program can work in a number of ways, no matter what values you want to instill in your children.

To incorporate your particular values into this system, you can go in a few different directions. You could simply add your specific values to the original twelve, and go on for however many months you like. Or swap out some of the values I have listed, and replace them with ones you feel are more important to you. Another way to go would be to take a closer look at the twelve values as they exist in this book and see where your values might be incorporated. For instance, leadership can be brought into Self-Respect Month. Cooperation could be a part of how you teach your children about respecting others. And loyalty can easily be discussed during Integrity Month and incorporated into the exercises. Always do whatever works best for your family.

For instance, in our case, we truly value love and family, yet they do not appear as specific values in our yearlong journey because I couldn't separate either of them from what we already do every day. Those values wind their way throughout every day of the year. The overall message of this book is to live each value genuinely, so though we do not focus a month on love per se, I no longer insist my kids "give Aunt Martha a big kiss" or "hug Uncle Fred." I let them express their love in whatever way feels appropriate and genuine to them.

I also value creativity and find that it is already a part of how we teach values because the exercises are a great expression of creativity for my entire family. So you may find that some of your values work this way too.

This journey can be started any time of the year, and you can do the values in any order that works for your family. We've now done this system with our children for three years, so we switch the values around as needed. For instance, if we feel that our kids need more help in being responsible, we simply move Commitment Month up in the line-up. It's a very flexible system.

The goal of this book is to get your children, ages five through about twelve years old, actively involved in three specific, fun, and meaningful exercises each month. These exercises will help you to impart your values in a way that will have a profound and lasting impression on your children. Though the idea of embarking on a yearlong journey with your family may seem daunting, in truth it typically will take no more than five minutes for the daily exercises, yet they are effective because you will do them every day, and the repetition will reinforce the value throughout the month and beyond. The weekly exercises take fifteen minutes or so, and they drive home a different aspect of each value. Finally, the one-time exercises wrap up each month with a final lesson, and they generally take about an hour. There is a chapter for each value, with step-by-step instructions on how to do the exercises, and variations to give your family flexibility as you experience each month. Several families besides my own are now on this journey as well, and I will touch on their experiences in each chapter.

Throughout the book, I use the terms "spouse" or "partner" when referring to parents. However, several single parents have experienced this program with their children as well. I use these terms strictly for ease of use and do not mean to discourage any family from participating.

As each month unfolds, you'll find that your children begin to understand why specific virtues are important to you and how to live them. As parents, you can share stories from your own lives, from before you had kids. Tell them about times in your lives when you have lived your values by showing gratitude, respect for others, integrity, compassion—any and all of the values that are important to you. If your kids are anything like ours, this will fascinate them, as sometimes it doesn't even occur to them that their parents *existed* before they came along! The best thing about sharing these stories with your kids is that they get to know you better. They'll begin to see you as more three-dimensional people, instead of just "parents." They'll realize that you truly believe in something, and they'll start to understand that you've actually been *living* as if you believe in something. So you're not just teaching them values; you're giving them a part of yourselves.

And by focusing on just one value a month, children have an opportunity to really explore what the value means to them. This isn't a system designed to program your child to say a rote "thank you" during Gratitude Month. Instead, it will help teach your child how to grow into a decent human being who understands on a deeper level what it truly means to be grateful for something and to express that gratitude sincerely.

Although this is a twelve-month program, the practice is an ongoing part of life, and you won't have to wait a year to start seeing results, as the families who are already using this system have found. Your children will start truly living your values every day, in significant and heartfelt ways that will stick with them for a lifetime.

Month One

GRATITUDE

Saying "thank you" and meaning it

Have you ever given a new toy to your daughter that you thought would absolutely thrill her only to get a lackluster response; or handed over a just-released video game to your son that left him completely underwhelmed? Sure, they said thank you and gave polite little smiles, but you could tell they weren't actually grateful. And you feel like you went to all that trouble for nothing. Maybe it's not that your kids are ungrateful. Maybe they don't really know what it's like to be genuinely grateful because you've never truly expected it of them before. This chapter can help you teach your kids how to experience true gratitude and to express it in a sincere way.

The Magic Words

Looking back at when my son was little, I realized that I had it all wrong when it came to teaching him about gratitude. I had equated hearing the words "Thank you" with being grateful. But I had completely missed the mark. Those times when my son did say those magic words were actually more a reflection of training, not teaching. And when he said nothing, like the time he received the blue T-shirt from my friend, it was clear even the training wasn't going so well.

One goal of Gratitude Month is to go beyond teaching your children to automatically say "Thank you" when someone gives them a gift, for instance. Because what is the point in saying the words if they have no meaning? Before we began Gratitude Month, I started consciously observing my kids to see if I could figure out where they were in terms of being grateful. Try it for a few days yourself. I think it's worth doing before getting started on this particular month. In our case, I noticed that sometimes my children seemed to be feeling thankful yet not expressing it to anyone, and at other times, they would say "Thank you" but there didn't seem to be any emotion behind it. There was clearly a disconnect. So, during Gratitude Month we wanted to make a connection between the feeling and the words—a connection that would be real and lasting.

To make that connection, start the month out by simply talking to your kids. And it should be a talk—never a lecture. The more you sound like you're lecturing, the more your kids will mentally turn the volume down. You're not going to accomplish anything if they're zoned out. So to begin, each month tell your kids what value you will be focusing on and why. For gratitude, at our house, my husband and I tell our kids that life isn't about what you have or don't have, but rather it's about being grateful for the things and experiences, even the challenges, that are part of your life.

Some children may feel a bit embarrassed when you start talking about gratitude, and they may need reassurance. They may think you consider them ungrateful. If that happens, let your kids know that you're not bringing up this value because of anything they lack, but rather because this value is important to you and you wanted to share it with them. Also, letting kids know that the whole family will be going through the month together really helps, because then it is a shared experience and a chance for everyone in the family to get to know each other a little better.

How Does It Feel to Be Grateful?

On the first day of Gratitude Month, you may want to ask your children what being thankful feels like to them. Is it about saying "Thank you?" Well, how do they feel when they say those words? My daughter, at five, wasn't quite able to connect the feeling to the words at first. That was a great starting point for us because we wanted to know what she felt like when she said those words to someone. And it turned out that sometimes she felt . . . pretty much nothing. That wasn't too surprising to us in a way. There was that disconnect. After all, we had spent so much time and effort insisting on those words without realizing what a meaningless experience it was for our children. So we talked with our daughter about how there is a great feeling that should go with the words "Thank you." That feeling is called gratitude. We explored what that would really feel like by asking her how she felt when she received presents on Christmas morning, or when I brought her favorite snack home from the store, or when just the two of us spent the day together. We just focused on the *feeling*. By talking to her it was clear that she understood the feeling on some level, but she hadn't realized (our fault) that she should be feeling it when she said those words . . . that the feeling and the words "match up."

Grace loves playing matching games, and she's really good at it, so she related to this concept. We went from there, explaining that in a matching game, if you only have one piece, like "Thank you," but you don't experience the accompanying gratitude, then you don't really have a "match." Or if you feel grateful, like when Grandma gives you one of her delicious, homemade chocolate chip cookies, but you don't say the words, you haven't made a "match" or a connection there either. And when you make that connection and your words match up with your feelings, you are being genuinely grateful. That's not only a good feeling for a young child like Grace, but when she expresses her sincere thanks to her grandma, for example, they share a moment that's real.

If you have an older child, you'll probably approach the first talk about gratitude a little differently. If your child already understands the connection between the feeling of gratitude, and the words expressing the feeling, you are able to take your discussion even further. You may talk about how it's easy to make a connection between a happy event, like a surprise stop at an ice cream shop, and that jubilant "Thanks, Mom!" that would probably follow. But what about when things don't look worthy of thanks? What if your older child was hoping to go swimming at the community pool and a thunderstorm ruined his plans? You might ask him if there is any room for gratitude there. Or what if your daughter's best friend moves out of town? What's there to be grateful for anyway? The idea is to help older children expand their understanding of gratitude. You don't need all the answers at this point. The month-long journey will help with that.

Here's what I use for this month's exercises, but feel free to check out the variations listed later, or come up with your own ideas.

Supplies for This Month's Exercises
- A large poster board in white or a light color
- Set of colorful markers
- A few sheets of card stock or construction paper for the one-time exercise

Daily Exercise: The Gratitude Board

On the first day of the month, your family should start to explore what you are grateful for with the Gratitude Board. This exercise only takes about five minutes each day, yet helps you and your kids find reasons to be grateful for the ordinary experiences—and even the challenges—in your everyday lives.

The Gratitude Board is simply a large poster board that you display this month in your kitchen, playroom, or anywhere that works for your family. Every night before bed, all members of your family should take a marker and write one thing that each of you are grateful for from that day. Your kids might write things like "We got to go to the park," or "I knew all my spelling words at school," or "Charlie gave me a cookie at lunch." What your children come up with may surprise you. After my son had been home from school with the flu for several days, he wrote, "I got to go to school today!"

Sounds simple enough, right? But what if the kids have had a miserable day and aren't feeling particularly thankful? Maybe your son got an unexpected poor grade on a test at school, or another girl left your daughter out of a game she wanted to play at recess and it affected their outlooks for the whole day. No worries . . . you can work with that. Encourage them to search for something positive in spite of everything. Did your son simply put away the test and think to himself that he should try harder next time rather than getting upset? Did your daughter find another child who had been left out and ask her to play? They can be thankful for that. They had a challenge and it was an opportunity to grow . . . to reach beyond what they usually expect of themselves. So they might, when pushed to go a little deeper, find something of meaning to be grateful for. That is what they should write on the Gratitude Board.

In my house, we always keep what we write short and simple, and we each try to use our favorite colored markers to help identify who wrote what. You can even draw pictures or put stickers on the Gratitude Board if they add to the feelings you are trying to convey.

Kate and Jeff, parents of an eleven-year-old daughter and seven-year-old son, focused on gratitude for a month. Kate was often surprised to read what her family wrote on the Gratitude Board. One day, after visiting a homeless shelter with their church group, Kate's daughter wrote that she was grateful that the shelter was there for people who needed it, and after studying with a math tutor, she wrote that she was grateful to be excited about math! Her son wrote that he was grateful for an unexpected visit from a friend. Kate appreciated the fact that her kids actually hugged and kissed each other and her husband was grateful for "eye-opening experiences." Writing things like this down every day on the Gratitude Board can help you see things that might otherwise be missed or taken for granted. Yet in fact, they are things that give us an opportunity to experience true gratitude.

Parents will also benefit from this exercise. Often, after a busy day at work, or even after a day off where I spent far too much time running errands, the message I write is "My daughter read a book to me." Or, "The whole family cuddled on the couch and watched a movie together." The wonderful thing about this is that my husband and I generally end up writing that we are grateful for our children and each other, and this allows our kids to notice that they are appreciated and that we are grateful for each other as a couple.

Your kids can look at the Gratitude Board all month and see how thankful you are for every moment you spend with your family. Not only do they see how much they mean to you, but they also get to know you a little better as they see the comments you write about your jobs, your extended families, and your friends.

Some Variations on the Gratitude Board

Some families prefer to use a dry erase board because they don't have a good place to display a large poster board. Every night, they just erase the previous day's items and move on. If your kids have access to the computer, you might prefer to post what you are grateful for on your family social networking page, or simply email your daily gratitude messages to everyone in your family. Or you and your kids might want to make the Gratitude Board on the computer. Have them design it themselves. The more involved the kids are, the more likely they are not only to stick with the exercise, but also to look forward to it. Maybe you would prefer to make a little family film and record messages each night that express gratitude. If you prefer to keep it really simple, just have everyone in the family say what they are grateful for at dinner each night, or at bedtime when you say good night. Do whatever works best for your family and you can't go wrong.

Weekly Exercise: Rewind

Once the daily exercise is in full swing, add a once-a-week activity to the mix. We typically do this every weekend during the month. We call this exercise Rewind and the goal is to help the children understand what it truly means to *receive*. So whereas the daily exercise asks you and your family to look back on your days and find things to be grateful for, this exercise focuses on what happens when you are actually given something. This is where you can strive to go beyond that rote "*Thaaank Youuuu*" we're used to hearing from kids and show them that there's a lot more to be thankful for than meets the eye.

Explain to your children that the moment someone gives them a gift (or hands them a sandwich for that matter) is really the end of the process, in a way. By "rewinding" the process, it helps them see when the act of giving really begins. Let's review this exercise using the example of my son Connor and the T-shirt.

When my friend saw that T-shirt in the store, she noticed it was blue, and thought about Connor, remembering that blue is his favorite color. I imagine she gave it some thought, compared it to a few other T-shirts, and made her decision. Then she probably stood in a long line, paid for it with money she earned working diligently at her job, brought it home, wrapped it, and gave it to my son. At the time, his insincere "Thank you" was utterly meaningless. But as we worked our way through Gratitude Month when he was older, we reminded him of that experience. We told him that when he receives a gift, it is about much more than that moment of opening it and seeing what's inside. It's about the *process*. And we have him "rewind" to the beginning of the process himself, imagining each step of the way and asking him to picture the person going through each thing: choosing the gift, waiting in line, etc. This way, as he goes back through the process, it helps him realize that the *giving* actually began long before he received the gift. We say, "Be grateful for the entire experience that brought you the gift." My husband and I also go through this exercise once a week this month with gifts we have received or even when someone hands us a simple glass of water. We do this not only to further illustrate for our kids how the process works, but also to remind ourselves not to take anything for granted.

Children as young as five years old can understand and imagine this process. Let's say you are explaining this exercise to your young daughter. Use an example of a toy she has recently received and really liked so she can differentiate her joy at getting the gift with whether she was feeling genuine gratitude for it. Go through the steps with her, "rewinding" the process so she can see that a lot of time and effort went into getting that toy to her. This can help her to understand that there is more to be grateful for than the toy alone. And though she may like this particular toy, ultimately, whether the gift is wanted or not has nothing to do with the gratitude you want her to feel. The point of this month is not about teaching kids to be grateful for "things" but rather to help them be grateful for the time, the kindness, the work, and the thoughtfulness that is *behind* the things. That's the part that really matters.

And remember that sandwich I mentioned earlier? When you hand your child lunch, ask him or her to look at everything on the plate and think about where it all came from and how it got to them. Rewind; think about the entire process. Think about the farmers who grew the food and the people who worked in the fields to pick the fruits and vegetables. That's back-breaking, exhausting work. Then the food was brought to the grocery store where you carefully selected it, checking freshness dates, and examining fruits and vegetables for ripeness and cans for dents. Then you bought the food, stood in line, and paid for it with money you earned working at your job. You carried those heavy bags of groceries from your car into the house and spent twenty minutes putting everything away. And then after all that, you made a nutritious lunch and handed it to your children. *That's* what you want them to be grateful for, and not in a guilt-inducing way, like "We did all of this for *you*. You should be so grateful." Not that at all. Rather, "Realize the journey this food went through to get to you and be grateful for the entire process."

Of course, you don't need to go through this explanation every single time. Too much of a good lesson, and most kids will stop listening. This exercise should be done once a week during Gratitude Month—and that's enough to make an impact on a child. It certainly did for my children. I now see them stopping and really looking at the food on their plates. I notice that when my daughter takes her plate, she looks directly at me and says, "Thanks, Mom" and she is genuinely smiling. That is far different from a rushed "Thank you" that comes from habit rather than genuine gratitude. Now, when my son says a prayer before dinner and thanks "the farmers who worked hard in the fields growing the grain for this delicious bread, and the people who picked the apples in our applesauce," we know that not only did we teach him something significant about gratitude, but we've also enriched his life in a way that will stay with him.

Our hope is that over time, our children will get beyond thinking about it and simply *experience* gratitude before they eat a meal. Although a prayer of thanks before eating is a beautiful thing to do, in some ways it can be just about the words if you are not actually feeling the gratitude.

And if you think about how meaningful it can be to stop and say a prayer before a meal, imagine the prayer without words. It is just a feeling, a silent and deep moment of gratitude to whatever higher power you believe in. That is the profound experience you are laying the groundwork for when you teach your children to stop before a meal and think about the entire process. Part of the message you are giving your children is simply to "stop." That way, the experience of the meal isn't lost. Though your family may be busy, this small act of stopping ever so briefly before a meal allows time for experiencing genuine gratitude.

Some Variations on Rewind:

For some children, especially those ages five or six, this exercise may seem overwhelming if there are too many steps. So it may help them to Rewind by only using two or three steps. For example, a simple and understandable process may be "an apple that was grown in a farmer's orchard was bought by my mom at the farmer's market." Or take out a piece of paper and draw a few pictures to illustrate the process (or have your child draw). Some kids are visual learners and this will help them to grasp the concept.

The main point you want to communicate with this exercise is that the blessings that come into our lives don't just magically appear. There is a process. And we want our children to learn to see and appreciate that process so that every gift, every toy, and every meal has more meaning to them and engenders true gratitude in their hearts rather than an automatic "Thank you." So as long as you are doing this exercise in a way that conveys this message, you are on the right track.

One-Time Exercise: The Thanks for Nothin' Letter

The one-time exercise happens at the end of the month precisely because your kids have had a chance to learn about gratitude, and are ready to do an exercise that is a little more practical. With this exercise, you want to go a little deeper, and find even more meaning in gratitude.

This exercise involves writing a thank-you letter. Not the standard, "thank-you" note written in response to receiving a gift, although I strongly encourage that as well. (I say "strongly encourage" rather than "insist" because we always want the gratitude to come from our children themselves, rather than from us, "through" them.) This letter is more than that, because it is not acknowledging a "thing." It is acknowledging a person, and how grateful we are to have them in our lives.

During Gratitude Month, you should talk to your children about how easy it is to take each other for granted, accepting love, friendship, and support from the people in your lives, without ever taking the time to thank them for everything they do. So do something very old fashioned and simple. Each member of your family should write a letter to someone you care about. In the letter, tell that person all the things you appreciate about them. It can be anyone in your lives—a neighbor, grandparent, teacher, aunt, uncle, or even a friend, sibling, or parent. The only caveat is that it not be someone's birthday, or a holiday, or a special day of any kind. It's a "just because" kind of thing.

Both our children chose to write their thank-you letters to their teachers, which was lovely, because they each had teachers who were so generous and kind. As my son wrote his letter, I noticed that he had written the word "very" several times, which I suspected was to fill up the page. When I asked him about it, he said "No, Mom. That's not what I'm doing. I just want her to know how grateful I am that she's my teacher. I'd like to put more "verys" but I'm running out of room." This helped me to get some perspective that I wasn't writing the note and it wasn't my sentiment being expressed. These notes were from my children, in their own words (misspellings and all) and they were written from the heart. And that is the point of the whole exercise.

Some Variations on the Thanks for Nothin' Letter:

Although I prefer the old-fashioned quality of a handwritten letter, you may decide that a phone call or even an e-mail is a more appropriate way for your family to express thanks. The main message of the exercise is to be grateful for something that is not concrete, because those are the kinds of thing that often go unnoticed and unappreciated.

Writing a simple thank-you letter in any format may seem like a small thing, but it encourages your children to be aware that they are receiving great gifts on a daily basis. Gifts of kindness, consideration, patience, humor, and wisdom. It is so easy to miss these, especially since we are living in such a consumer-oriented society where children are encouraged to want one "thing" after another. This one-time exercise focuses on a more novel idea. Simply appreciating someone for who they are, and not a gift they have given or a meal they have made, brings a little bit more richness to the experience of gratitude. And again, by participating in the exercise ourselves, it gives us the opportunity to do something we otherwise probably wouldn't do . . . stop and take the time to thank someone special in our own lives.

This brings me to another important part of Gratitude Month in our house. We are the kind of family who says "I love you" all the time. As parents, we make a special effort to let our children know we are grateful for them, for their personalities, for their kindness and gentleness, for their silliness and humor, and for everything that makes them unique. We used to be so focused on just getting our kids to say "thank you" that we often forgot to express it ourselves. This month is not just about teaching our children. It is also about reminding ourselves as a couple to really think about how blessed we are to have each other, and to have our wonderful children. This enriches our lives as individuals, of course, because we are living what is important to us, and experiencing gratitude is very important to us. And we certainly want to be good examples to our children—as people who are truly "walking the walk" and not just "talking the talk." But it isn't enough, as we found out, to simply try to be an example. At least not for us. I suspect other families are experiencing the same thing. But by taking an entire month to really focus on gratitude and to do the exercises together, we have seen our children make that crucial connection between saying "Thank you" and genuinely feeling gratitude. Being grateful has become a part of who they are.

So in addition to doing all the talking, teaching, and exercises each month, we also embrace and cherish these values as parents and as individuals. When you do this as a parent, and your children witness the gratitude you have for each of them and for your spouse or partner, they can better understand who you are as people. They can get to know you, not just as parents, but as people who are doing the best they can to live and teach what is most important to them.

Staying Power

I have seen firsthand the changes in my both of my children after Gratitude Month. For instance, long after we had focused on gratitude, my children and I were driving along a quiet street and we noticed that daffodils were starting to bloom in almost every front yard we passed. After a particularly long and icy winter, this was indeed a sight for sore eyes. As we passed each house, my son or daughter would gleefully shout out "Look, Mom, over there . . . more daffodils!" I pointed out to the kids that we should be very thankful for these lovely flowers. "I know, mom," my daughter said. "You don't need to tell us. It's the gift of daffodils!"

And my son recently showed how Gratitude Month has made an impact on him. When we told him about an upcoming trip to Rome—a really big deal for our family—and mentioned that we would be visiting the Trevi Fountain so he could make a wish, he said something that really touched my heart. "But mom, if I was in Rome at the Trevi Fountain, what more could I possibly wish for?"

Thinking Beyond "Thank You"

As you move on to the next month and start focusing on the next value, how can you continue to foster gratitude in your children? The best way is to continue to live the lessons of Gratitude Month as a family. For one thing, though you won't be formally using a Gratitude Board next month, you should still regularly talk about things that you are grateful for, and encourage your kids to do the same. And as a parent, you can reinforce the lessons learned in the Rewind exercise by openly appreciating the process, and not just the results, of what your kids do. For instance, if your daughter comes home with an "A" on her report card, acknowledge and appreciate the process—all the work and effort that went in to getting that "A"—rather than just focusing on the grade itself. Also emphasize to your children that you want them to be grateful people who appreciate and acknowledge the obvious and the not-so-obvious gifts in their lives.

And by the way, don't be discouraged if your children don't always say thank you when they get a gift or you hand them a bowl of ice cream. For kids, figuring out that *being grateful* actually matters more to their parents than *saying thank you* may take some adjustments. So the next time your children accept that gift, or dessert, or whatever it is, and you don't hear those magic words, relax. You can do something to help them start to "get it." Don't fall into the trap of repeating that worn out question "Hey, what do you say?" hoping to prompt a "Thank you." Instead, ask your child, "How do you feel right now?" If they say they feel good or happy or even like they might want to cry, that's okay. You're not pushing them to say something insincere. You're giving them the chance to think about how they feel and then to connect—on their own—how they want to express that feeling. The words will come. But the feeling is more important. And when your child is able to make that connection, you won't have to remind them about the feeling or the words anymore. It will just come naturally.

Month Two

SELF-RESPECT

The balance between confidence and humility

If children respect themselves, they can do just about anything in their lives. Think about how many people you know who have held themselves back from accomplishing things, not because they didn't have an education, opportunities, or skills, but because they didn't love themselves, or believe in themselves enough to go for it. It happens all the time. There are enough obstacles in life without your children having to struggle to get past the ones they put in their own way. That's why focusing on self-respect for a month with your kids can be crucial for them.

The S Word

Parents can pick up a few reminders along the way, too. Too often, we are the ones putting ourselves down. I know. It's happened to me. But we have to do our best not to let those negative messages gain momentum in our lives. Have you ever had one of those mornings when you're trying to leave the house, get your kids to school, and yourself to work, and you're running late? You know, your purse is over one shoulder, your laptop over the other, and your hands are full carrying your son's science project or a plate of cupcakes for your daughter's class. And as you're attempting to maneuver all that out the door, you suddenly realize you haven't the slightest clue where your keys are. "Ugggggggghhhhh! I am so stupid!!!" just pops out of your mouth before you have a chance to stop it. Then you realize your kids are standing right there, taking it all in.

Something like that happened to me several months ago, and my daughter looked up in shock and said, "You just said the "S" word!" (In our house "stupid" *is* the S word.) And my son quickly came to my defense. "Hey mom, don't say that!" Of course, I backtracked right away and told them I was just frustrated and I didn't mean it, and that was true. I didn't mean it. I don't think I'm stupid at all. Disorganized, hurried, absent-minded, hungry, frazzled, sleep deprived—all those things, but not stupid. Although I may silently "yell" at myself a bit when I make a mistake, my sense of self is never in question. It made me wonder then, if I have a healthy sense of self-respect, why I put myself down, right in front of my children. I wonder if those kinds of messages are just so pervasive in everyday life that I adopted that self-deprecating talk without even knowing it. Maybe it's just more socially acceptable to blurt out "I'm a complete mess" than to say, "I'm really keeping it together. Yay me!"

No matter what the reason, if we parents are putting ourselves down, it has to stop, not only for our own sake, but also for the erroneous message we may be sending to our children. Many kids already feel like they are not "good enough," so if they see their parents expressing the same kinds of feelings, it may reinforce their own insecurities. As parents, we should do everything we can to show our children what healthy self-respect looks like.

The challenge with self-respect is that it's not something we can just give to our kids, or to anyone else for that matter. We can encourage it, try to develop it, and acknowledge it when we see it, but we can't make it happen. Boy, is that frustrating. What we can do is to start laying the groundwork for a healthy sense of self in our children.

One of our goals during this month is to show our kids that to us, self-respect is the foundation upon which they can build their lives, and it goes beyond self-esteem. So much of what they see on TV, in the movies, and even down the block is geared toward building self-esteem, which on the surface, seems wonderful. But it is possible to go too far. If your kids are involved in sports, then they've probably brought home a trophy or two, or seven for that matter. Sometimes that's all from one competition! Do adults think their egos are so fragile that kids can't face the fact that they may not be the best little league player, or gymnast, or swimmer out there? And by always "cushioning their fall" are we really doing them any favors? If we are creating self-esteem with this approach, it is fleeting. Self-respect goes so much deeper than that.

Also, if everyone "wins," how can children see themselves as individuals who excel at some things but not others? The idea of individuality gets a bit lost in this approach. As a parent, I want my kids to *celebrate* their individuality rather than simply try to fit in with what everyone else is doing.

So to start out Self-Respect Month, simply have a conversation with your children about what it means to respect themselves. Self-respect is loving yourself and knowing that you have value as the unique person you are, and that your worth is never tied to a specific accomplishment or material object. It has nothing to do with what other people think of you. Nothing whatsoever. As much as it pains me to say it, that would include parents. Of course, you should still praise your children. You can't help but be enthusiastic about their accomplishments, but try to step back to give them room to feel good about themselves, separate and apart from what you think. For one thing, aren't we putting too much pressure on our kids if we always make them feel like they are "the best"? And you don't want your children to look for their sense of self in you or anyone else but themselves, because frankly, they won't find it anywhere else. It is more important that your children truly learn to "know who they are" and trust that knowledge like a touchstone on which they can rely unfailingly. And speaking of failure, in my family, we encourage it. When you think about it, what could be better for true self-respect than failure? Because if a child learns how to recoup after a failure, then he knows what it is genuinely like to feel good about himself. For us, that is how children can start to go beyond self-esteem to self-respect.

Roots of Self-Respect

For a lesson in self-respect, I took my children into our backyard where there is a very old, very tall evergreen tree. We really looked at the tree and noticed its imperfections—the missing branches that were probably blown off during a bad storm, the patches of brown needles here and there, and the fact that it doesn't go up perfectly straight. Then I said to my kids, "It's still here and it will be here for a very long time. Why do you think that is?" They took a good, long look at the tree, starting at the top and working their eyes down to the ground. At that point, my son said "The roots, mom." I agreed. I told my kids that the tree has been nourished by rainwater and by the warm rays of the sun all these years, much as a child is nurtured by the encouragement, support, and love of his parents. Because of the tree's strong roots, it is still growing strong and healthy despite all the difficult conditions it has endured.

When beginning Self-Respect Month, consider using the same example with your children. After all, like the tree, we rely on our own strong "roots" when life brings difficult situations. Obstacles come into our lives, and we inevitably make mistakes and even fail at things that are important to us. But if we have a strong sense of who we are, if we have love and respect for ourselves, then like that old evergreen, we too can withstand the challenges life sends our way. You can also have your children look around at other trees and see that each one is individual and unique, like people are. No one tree is better or worse than any other. They each have value.

If you have younger children, consider another image they may relate to. For example, if your children like going to the park, ask them to visualize the seesaw for a moment. When there are two children about the same size, that seesaw works really well and both kids have fun. But when there is one small child, and another much bigger child trying to play on the seesaw, it just doesn't work. You need balance. That's how self-respect works. You throw off the balance if you think so much of yourself that you look down on someone else, and you have the same issue if you're always on the bottom, looking up at other people while you belittle yourself. If you can find your balance between those two extremes, that's how self-respect feels. When I explained that concept to my daughter, she said, "I get it mom. Never think you're better than anyone or badder than anyone." From the mouths of babes.

After starting to talk with your kids about self-respect, you are ready to start the exercises for this month. Through the exercises, you will explore the balance between confidence and humility, and the concept that each child is an individual worthy of the many blessings they have been given. Beyond that, they are also worthy of the challenges and even the hardships they will face in their lives. In other words, they are up to the task of living a full life with varied and unexpected experiences.

Supplies for This Month's Exercises:

- None are needed unless you want to write out your daily mantra for the first exercise and post it for your family to see every day.

Daily Exercise: Self-Respect Mantra

When my mother was a child growing up on a small farm in Ireland, her mother would often repeat a simple, but profound saying about self-respect: "You may be no better than anyone else, but no one is better than you." Those straightforward words may seem out of place in our competitive society, where getting ahead and being perceived as better than others is often the goal. But I believe those words and have lived by them. The wonderful thing about this mantra is that it is rooted in balance. It isn't about building yourself up at the expense of others, nor is it about humbling yourself to the point of becoming a doormat. It's about honoring yourself as an individual and it's about true self-respect.

Each morning during Self-Respect Month ask everyone in your family to say the words handed down by my grandmother as their simple daily exercise, or choose a mantra of your own. Nora and her husband, Eli, focused on self-respect with their eight-year-old daughter. They used my grandmother's mantra and found that when their daughter said it every day it was "a great reminder to her to remain proud and confident, yet humble." If you decide to choose your own mantra, feel free to write one that embodies your own beliefs about self-respect or find a meaningful quote that inspires you. Some ideas:

- "If you put a small value on yourself, rest assured the world will not raise your price."—Unknown
- "No one can make you feel inferior without your consent."—Eleanor Roosevelt
- "That you may retain your self-respect, it is better to displease the people by doing what you know is right, than to temporarily please them by doing what you know is wrong."—William J. H. Boetcker, religious leader
- "Respect yourself and others will respect you."—Confucius, Chinese philosopher
- "We are all something, but none of us are everything."—Blaise Pascal, French mathematician and philosopher

Variations on the Self-Respect Mantra:

You may prefer to use different quotes throughout the month rather than the same one every day. Each member of the family could come up with an idea and the family could take turns saying the different mantras. Or if you do use one mantra, your kids might enjoy creating artwork to express it. In that case, your whole family could see and be inspired by your child's artwork throughout the month. And if you think the drawing or painting is fantastic, remember to consider restraining your enthusiasm just enough to allow room for your child to feel good about himself regardless of what you think. That way your child can feel proud of the artwork because he knows he did a good job without the pressure of thinking he's the next Picasso.

Weekly Exercise: Make a Choice about Your Inner Voice

How many times have you heard your own children disparage themselves in a way they would never do to another child? Unfortunately, most parents hear this at one time or another. The goal of this exercise is to teach your children that words are powerful, and that all of us should "speak" to ourselves with acceptance and dignity. Ultimately, what others think of us is nowhere near as powerful as what we think of ourselves. As parents, we need to show our children that the way they "speak" to themselves sets the tone for the way they see themselves in the world. Do they have the potential to be powerful and to make a difference? If so, do they talk to themselves in a way that's worthy of that image or do they downplay their abilities and therefore minimize the contributions they could make to the world?

You undoubtedly want your children to honor and believe in themselves as worthwhile people, faults and all. So when they fail at something, this exercise helps to separate that failure from who the child is as a person. In other words, their actions or their shortcomings do not define them. They should still love themselves, regardless of their mistakes and failures. In order to drive this point home, once a week during this month, ask each of your children to imagine a scenario where they feel they have not lived up to their own expectations, or have "failed" someone else. You can participate with them by sharing examples of when this has happened in your own life, or simply by responding to the comments they make about themselves in whatever situations they talk about. It could be something that has already happened in their lives recently, or they can make it up. If they can't come up with anything, you can provide the situation, such as missing a word in an early round of the spelling bee at school, sleeping through the alarm and being late for a play date with a friend, or breaking grandma's favorite vase in her living room because they were throwing cushions around. Ask them what is the very first thing they would say to themselves. They might respond with some variations of "I'm so stupid!" "I'm always late!" or "Why am I so clumsy all the time?" From there, ask them to imagine themselves saying those same words to a friend at school, or to each other, or even to you. When my family did this exercise, my son said that he would never, ever call me stupid because it was mean and disrespectful, and he loved me too much to talk to me like that. I responded that he should love himself just as much and he shouldn't be mean or disrespectful to himself because he is entitled to the same dignity and respect he would give me. Then I asked him how he would feel if *I* was the one saying he was stupid for missing a word in a spelling bee. He couldn't imagine that I would talk to him that way because he said it would be cruel. Exactly.

Many of us are familiar with the Golden Rule, to "treat others as you want them to treat you." We'll revisit that concept next month when learning about respecting others. But for this month, use the Golden Rule as a springboard for how each of us should be treated. Discuss how you should also try to live by what my son has dubbed The Rainbow Rule: "Treat yourself as well as you treat other people."

Variations on Make a Choice about Your Inner Voice:

You may prefer to use a mirror for this exercise, so that, for example, your son is looking at himself while saying the words aloud. Or if your kids are self-conscious, you can act out a scenario two ways for your children. The first time, show your children how not to talk to themselves about a mistake, and the second time, show them how to respond to that same situation in a way that shows self-respect. Or, for example, have your daughter imagine a situation in which she has achieved a great triumph and ask her to share what she would say to herself. If she talks to herself in a way that elevates her so much that she sees herself as above others, we are not achieving the goal of true self-respect, which does not come at the expense of how we view or treat others. Through this exercise and throughout the month we are continuing to strive for that balance between confidence and humility.

One-Time Exercise: Give It Your Best (or Worst) Shot

At the end of the month, take the time to explore the concept of perfection. After all, no one is perfect. And as parents, we shouldn't expect our children to waste their time and energy in search of this elusive goal. It's not that perfection can't exist, necessarily. We have all experienced moments of perfection—even entire days that just stand out in our mind as being absolutely sublime. But people are not perfect, and your children need to accept and love themselves as they are, faults and all. So with this exercise, give your children the opportunity to see that they shouldn't have unrealistic expectations for themselves.

A fun way to do this is to give them the chance to do something they've never done before, and join them! Rock climbing, ice skating, bowling, or modern dance—anything new will work, especially if it's something physical and potentially silly. It's okay if they get embarrassed when they try something new like this. What a great opportunity to give themselves a break, to go easy on their egos, and just have fun being bad at something! After all, what's wrong with being bad at something? Isn't that what learning and practice are for? And if it turns out that they're pretty good at it, how cool is that? Because that shows them that they may be good at all kinds of things if they only try. When their summer camp teacher asks for a volunteer to be the first to try playing the bongos, don't you want your kids to jump up and say, "I'll try it!"? It doesn't matter if they're good at it. What matters is that they have the confidence to *try* to succeed, and the willingness to fail.

Parents Nora and Eli tried this exercise with their eight-year-old daughter, and mentioned that she is great at athletics, but was afraid to get up in front of an audience. During Self-Respect Month, their daughter was able to try karaoke. She was nervous but found she was quickly able to put her anxiety aside, and she didn't care how she sounded. She just had fun!

Variations on Give It Your Best (or Worst) Shot:

For a younger child who might be intimidated by trying a brand new thing, simply have him go to a familiar activity and try to build on it. For example, if your child likes to draw, you could introduce a new medium, like oil paints, instead of crayons. Or, instead of drawing a picture on a piece of paper, you could go outside in the driveway and create a life-sized picture with colorful chalk. Or if you typically are the one to make a snack, maybe your child could take on that responsibility himself. It can be anything that allows him to try something he hasn't done before. Your children may also be encouraged by seeing you try something new. It could be as simple as taking on a new recipe you've never attempted before. This is a great way to take on this challenge together.

These lessons are never meant to be overwhelming, so if the whole idea of this exercise is too intimidating to your child, try getting out a piece of cardstock or construction paper. Ask your child to write his or her name prominently at the top of the page. Then have them fill up the page with qualities they would most like to see in themselves. So for a little girl named Keisha, she would imagine a sentence like, "Keisha would like to be . . . " and then she would fill in the blank with as many qualities as she could think of, writing them all over the page. She might write things like courageous, friendly, kind, funny, admired, respected, and loved. Then, mom or dad would write the word "is" after her name. So, Keisha "is" courageous, funny, admired, and so on. Simply post this somewhere she will see it every day and encourage your child to realize that those qualities are already in her. If she isn't able to see those qualities in herself yet, ask her to read the paper aloud every day to help her realize that she can be the person she wants to be.

Staying Power

After my family experienced Self-Respect Month, I was happy to see that the lessons really stayed with my kids. My daughter would sometimes put herself down after losing a game, but now I hear her say, "Oh well. I did my best." And my son wrote his own mantra that is personal to him. It helps him to let go of past mistakes so he can focus on the future.

To keep instilling the lessons of Self-Respect Month, be open to trying new experiences as individuals and together as a family. Seek them out. And remember, there is no pressure whatsoever to be good, just have fun! To reinforce self-respect every day, post your family's mantra where everyone can see it, like on the inside of the door you use as you leave your house. That way you'll notice it as you head off to start your day at work or school. It's a subtle but powerful reminder of how you should see yourselves in the world.

As situations arise where you or your kids feel that you have failed at something, try to make a positive choice about how you each "talk" to yourselves. For instance, if your young daughter loses at checkers and says something negative like, "I'm not good at anything!" take the time to talk to her about the importance of self-respect. Remind her that it has nothing to do with being perfect. She'll probably disagree with you. After all, what kid doesn't want to be perfect? Well, ask her to imagine going to a place I like to call "Planet Perfect." Sounds idyllic right? Well, maybe. On Planet Perfect, there would be no TV, no computers, no video games—in fact, no technology of any kind. Why not? Well, in order to have technology you must have inventors. And inventors need to make lots and lots of mistakes, which, of course, would never happen on Planet Perfect. I imagine everyone there looks the same and dresses the same because creativity isn't born of perfection either. It comes from a sense of individuality and a willingness to go out on a limb. You can imagine the barren landscape on this planet because of the "perfect" sunny weather every day. Without rain, there are no trees or green grass or flowers . . . well, you get the picture. I think at this point your child will start to understand that perfection is not all it's cracked up to be.

But I know—there might be days when even you as a parent feel like packing up and moving to your own version of Planet Perfect. Who can blame you? You might imagine a place where your job is ideal and you are in perfect shape. That's certainly tempting. But if we as parents can learn to accept ourselves and embrace our imperfections with love and a sense of humor, we don't need any kind of Planet Perfect. By doing our best to raise children who respect themselves, we will be making the world a better place. Not a perfect place—a better one. And that's the whole point.

Month Three
RESPECT FOR OTHERS

Living the Golden Rule

Respect for others is one of those values that our children can appear to have, when in fact they are not really experiencing it at all. You know, they might be calling their teacher "Miss Jackson," but rolling their eyes when she's not looking. Or they could be saying the magic word—please—because they've learned that if they don't say it, they won't get that cookie or piece of cake. But they may not be saying it out of genuine respect. This year of teaching values to your kids is all about getting past those surface niceties to the deeper, genuine feeling—in this case, respect for others. Sure, good manners are wonderful, but if it's all about just saying the words, and not about the accompanying respect, then it has no meaning. And respecting others should have a great deal of meaning. That's what this month is all about.

For instance, one day a few years ago, my husband and I attended an open house at a school we were considering for our children. Or, more accurately, I should say the school was considering our kids.

At one point, a school administrator standing nearby instructed us to get into small groups. He then sat down with our group and gave us his spiel about the school. He touted the strengths of various academic programs, mentioned extra-curricular activities available in the coming year, and described a diverse student population with children of many ethnic, religious, and racial backgrounds. He pointed out that their school worked so well because they strongly encouraged an atmosphere of tolerance. I raised my hand and pointed out that in my house we don't want our children to *tolerate* people from other cultures. We want our children to *celebrate* them. He was none too happy with the distinction. But to be fair, maybe that's what he meant. Perhaps that's what the word tolerance has come to mean to some people. But if you are trying to convey the message that you embrace everyone then why not say, "embrace"? Words are powerful. And as long as there is a shred of the definition of tolerance being associated with enduring the presence of, or putting up with other people, I'm not comfortable with it.

In today's society, "tolerance" is lauded as if it is a great achievement. But imagine saying the words "I tolerate you" to another person. There is no respect in that statement. Of course, it's better than hatred and persecution. But it's a very long way from acceptance, love, and genuine respect for others. Why aren't we aiming for that? Tolerance would have made a good first step, but it seems that in many ways we have simply stopped there, and that's not nearly enough.

So we do not allow the concept of tolerance in our home because it is much too low of a goal. We refuse to "tolerate" another person because he or she is of a different race, religion, ethnic background, or is disabled, short, tall, old, young, whatever it might be. A human being deserves better than tolerance. A human being is entitled to respect, and that's what Respect for Others Month is all about. Respect, not tolerance, is our starting point and we can go up from there.

Respect Starts at Home

Children learn how to respect others from their own experience with self-respect and from the way people are treated within their own families. Through Self-Respect Month, you have given your children the groundwork for self-respect, though certainly it is an ongoing process. This month, you should focus on providing them with an environment that fosters respect for others. And just like when they go out into the world, tolerance for each other isn't enough.

In my family, our kids are five years apart, different genders, and very different people. Sometimes they drive each other, and us, crazy. There are times when they just do not get along.

"Mom, Connor is in my room without my permission!"

"Oh yeah, well I only went in there because she took my book and I want it back!"

Does this sound familiar? We used to get this kind of stuff all the time with our kids, and it still happens from time to time, but much less often now that we have focused on respect for others. Respect starts at home, and in our house, that means we start with the basics. Just as in previous months, we want to make the concept of respecting others real and concrete, rather than some abstract idea that sounds good but they don't really "get."

When you have that first conversation about respect at the beginning of the month, start by talking about what your family believes respect is.

To me, respect often starts with connection. I tell my kids that one way to be respectful to someone else is to try to connect with that person in some way. It may only be a smile, brief eye contact, or a pleasant word. When it comes to respect, it all matters.

If you identify with this sentiment, make a special point of finding real and practical ways to show your children how to make that connection appropriately. If you're at the local pancake house with your family and the waitress comes over to take your order, you can look down at your menus and place your orders without ever really acknowledging that there's a person standing there waiting on you. Or each of you can look the waitress in the eyes, smile and say hello, and place your orders politely. This shows your children that just going out for pancakes is an opportunity to treat another human being with respect.

Throughout the month, you should continue to talk to your children about the very basics of respecting other people, such as using good manners, knocking before entering someone's room, asking before borrowing someone's belongings, and so on. But this is only the beginning of what it means to respect other people. Make it a goal to try to instill in your children why these things are important. To respect others is to honor their humanity. That is a very powerful thing for a child, or anyone, to do. Although that is a huge concept, especially for a child, do your best to break it down to an everyday level so they can relate to it and hopefully understand it.

For example, my husband and I asked our daughter how she felt when her brother went into her room without asking, and we gave our son the same chance to talk about how he felt when his sister took one of his favorite books without checking with him. Both kids say they felt awful, although not because of what they did, but because of what was done to them. Well, that's a start. It feels terrible to be disrespected. This is a good time to bring up The Golden Rule again. "Treat people as you would want them to treat you." I tell my kids that respect is a two-way street and both of them need to take responsibility for how they disrespected each other.

This is a good way to begin a discussion about point of view. When siblings argue, each child may feel justified in their actions, because from their point of view, they had been wronged. But the real cause for concern is when someone crosses the line from respect to disrespect. The daily exercise in Respect for Others Month is the perfect opportunity for children to better understand what respectful and disrespectful behavior actually looks like.

Supplies for This Month's Exercises

- The daily exercise can be done without tiles, but if you're doing it as we do, you'll need enough light-colored, 4-inch by 4-inch tiles for each day of the month. We bought thirty (and a few extra) for $1.12 each at our local hardware store, so we spent about $35 total. Other families have done this exercise more cost effectively by using alternate materials like construction paper, card stock, or index cards.

- Permanent markers in various colors.
- If using tiles, buy adhesive felt backing from the craft store. *An important tip if you are using tiles: When all the tiles are finished, you may want to spray them with a sealer from the hardware store because we have found that "permanent" markers aren't exactly permanent on tiles!*
- One 8-inch by 10-inch piece of paper or cardstock.
- A picture frame suitable for an 8-inch by 10-inch piece of paper.

Please note that if you choose to do it like my family does, the first exercise has more preparation time than the typical daily exercise, but once you start, it will usually take less than ten minutes a day.

Daily Exercise: Respect Tiles

On the first day of Respect for Others Month, sit down with your children and work together to come up with several ideas of how you can show respect to each other, and to everyone you encounter in your lives. There is only one guideline. Don't use the word "respect" when describing how to be respectful. That helps to make the concept less vague and abstract. So if your children suggest, "Respect the teacher," ask them how they could do that. Then they can be more specific, like "Raise your hand in school" or "Pay attention when the teacher is talking." Those things are more concrete and show respect to the teacher.

When you first start this exercise, encourage the kids to dominate the discussion because it's important to see what

Month Three

they'll come up with without too much influence from parents. Of course, since it is a family exercise, after a while, grownups should throw their thoughts in as well. Have someone in the family write down all the ideas and then together pick the top thirty. Now the creativity begins.

Give the kids several permanent markers in various colors and have them write on the tiles, which will serve as visual representations of the thirty ideas you've chosen. You may be surprised to see how creative they are. Initially, I thought my children would stick to writing down just the words, like "Return what you borrow," but once they started working on the tiles, they quickly decided to decorate them, and in some cases, illustrate them as well. For instance, my daughter felt that it is disrespectful to grab something out of someone else's hands. She made a respect tile with the words "Don't grab!" and a drawing of a stop sign. My son felt that one way to show respect to another person is simply to listen to them, so he created a respect tile with the word "Listen!" on it over a fairly elaborate picture of an ear, earring and all.

One of the best things about the day we made these tiles was the way my kids cooperated with each other. I had provided a package of permanent markers with several different colors, but there was only one marker of each color so they had to share. Connor would say to his sister, "Excuse me, would you please pass the purple marker?" And Grace would reply "Sure. May I have the green one?" They would then say "Thanks" as they handed the markers back and forth to each other. And they weren't being sarcastic! I never said a word to them about being respectful to each other while we did the exercise. They just figured it out on their own, which really turned it up a notch. They were already "getting it," and we had barely started Respect for Others Month. How cool is that?

After your kids have finished decorating the tiles, adhere the felt pieces to the backs and then spray them with sealer, if you choose to. Gently place them in an old pillowcase, and starting the next morning, have one of the kids carefully pull out a tile. One day, the tile may be "Don't interrupt when someone is speaking." That day, make a point of politely saying "Excuse me" after your child has finished talking and point out to her that you are doing that because it shows respect. Then let your daughter know that you are going to demonstrate the opposite of that respectful behavior. A few minutes later, interrupt her several times when she's trying to talk, and when she inevitably says "Hey!" ask her how she feels about it. She may say that it makes her feel frustrated. Point out that you have crossed the line from being respectful by waiting to talk and saying "excuse me," to being disrespectful by interrupting her. It's important to make the distinction as clearly as possible, so your kids will think twice before crossing that imaginary, but significant, line from respect to disrespect. Encourage your kids to practice the specific respectful skill—like not interrupting—on that particular day as well.

By the way, this exercise is not meant to encourage parents to actually *be* disrespectful to their children. Rather, the goal is to help kids understand how it might feel to be on the receiving end of disrespect in the context of an exercise so that they will be more sensitive to how they treat others.

Also, keep in mind that the idea of crossing the line as an example of what *not* to do seems to work well for older kids but might be a bit confusing for a younger child, who may do better with a simple explanation, rather than a demonstration of disrespect. For a younger child, it may be best to point out that if you did something disrespectful, such as not knocking on their door, for example, that would be crossing the line, and therefore you *didn't* do that behavior. Or you may even want to get a long ribbon or jump rope and place it on the floor. Use it to represent the "line" that you don't want your kids to cross. Stand on one side of the line and act out the respectful behavior like "knocking before entering." Then dramatically step over the ribbon or jump rope and act out the disrespectful behavior by pretending to barge into your child's room. Talk about how each behavior would make your child feel and reinforce how appropriate knocking before entering is. The goal here is to point out to your kids that they shouldn't cross that line into disrespect. Use the technique for this exercise that works best for your kids.

It's also very important to let your kids know that when someone crosses the line into disrespecting them, they need to say so. For example, when I do this exercise and interrupt my daughter, I encourage her to say something like "You've crossed the line into being disrespectful. I need to be treated with respect. Please don't interrupt." It may sound a bit formal, but instead of feeling frustrated by the disrespect, my kids now have that visual idea of someone crossing an unacceptable line. Once that line has been crossed, they have a structure for expressing their feelings about being disrespected. This has been great for my kids as siblings, so situations don't typically escalate as they used to.

Another day during Respect for Others Month, the tile might be "Don't borrow without permission." That day encourage your children to borrow from each other after asking permission in a respectful way. Make a point of borrowing things from your kids after politely asking to do so, and point out to them that you are being respectful. Then, only if it's appropriate for your children, let them know that you are going to borrow something from them without their permission. This is another chance to point out the difference between respectful and disrespectful behavior. Make sure your child sees you "borrowing" something from him without asking. When he inevitably asks you to stop, encourage him to tell you how he feels when you crossed the line into being disrespectful. An important point here is that only the grownups get to cross the line in this exercise. And you may find that you don't have to do that every day if they pick up the idea quickly. Ideally, it should only take a few times. At that point, you can shift your focus to showing your children the respectful behavior only.

The most important thing is that children actually get experience at being respectful each day this month. It may sound very simple, but it works because essentially they are "practicing" being respectful one skill at a time. And since they have looked at the other side of the coin—disrespect—they learn to make the distinction between the two.

The daily exercise also reinforces both aspects of respect . . . being *respectful* and being *respected.* Since each child has a chance to practice the respectful habit, and have others in the family practice being respectful to them, the respect comes full circle.

At the end of the month, you'll have thirty or so respect tiles in circulation. In my house, we use them as coasters and generally rotate them randomly in the kitchen and family room as subtle reinforcement of those respectful habits.

Variations on Respect Tiles:

If you're handy, smaller 2-inch by 2-inch tiles can be used and then placed together and grouted to make an interesting trivet. Or create your respect tiles using any material that works for your family. You could use cardstock or construction paper to create a collage of ways to be respectful. Or take digital photos of your family doing respectful things and put the pictures up around your house or in sequence in your computer. Add music if you want!

If you need some inspiration for what to put on your family's respect tiles, here are several idea to get you started.

- Say "Please" sincerely
- Don't interrupt
- Don't play music too loudly
- Refrain from sarcasm
- Don't stare at someone who looks different
- Flush the toilet!
- Don't gossip
- Obey your parents without arguing or bargaining
- Wait your turn
- Laugh with people, not at them
- Have good eye contact
- Say "Excuse me" politely
- Don't point
- Encourage others
- Don't call anyone a name
- Play gently with others' toys
- Clean up after yourself
- Tell the truth

- Hold doors open for others
- Recycle to honor the Earth
- Don't yell "Hey Mom!" from another room
- Be a good sport
- Don't insult anyone
- Clear your plate after meals
- Go the "extra mile" for others
- In public, only use your cell phone if you have to
- Be sensitive to others' feelings
- Don't talk back or sass
- Don't use bad language
- Keep your hands (and feet) to yourself!
- Be responsible
- Dress nicely for religious services
- Don't talk at the movies
- Be on time
- Be fair
- Follow rules
- Don't judge anyone
- Don't be bossy
- Keep your room clean
- Use your "inside voice" inside
- Use good hygiene
- Don't exclude disabled classmates in games—find a way to play together
- Use titles like "Mr. or "Mrs."
- Give up your seat if someone is standing
- Don't judge a book by its cover (Give people a chance!)

Many of these suggestions on how to be respectful come from parents Happi and Jerry who recently experienced

Respect for Others Month with their two sons, ages three and seven. Their three year old may be too young to appreciate the lessons of this exercise but he can be included in a way that is age appropriate so he doesn't feel excluded. Little ones don't like to be left out! Happi and her husband do this exercise in a way that works best for their children, by writing the values on strips of paper and placing all the strips in a glass bowl on the dinner table. One evening, they pulled the piece of paper with "Knock before entering someone's house or room." At that moment, much to their surprise, some neighborhood kids who are always welcome in their house just barged in without knocking while they were eating dinner! Apparently they felt a little too comfortable in Happi and Jerry's house. It was a perfect teaching moment, not only for their two sons, but for the neighborhood kids as well. They left once they realized it was dinnertime, but the windows were open and apparently they heard Happi talking to her sons about how barging in without knocking is disrespectful. So now they knock when they come over!

Weekly Exercise: Expand Your Horizons

One of the goals each month is for children to experience the value you are focusing on as deeply as possible. When it comes to respect, you should make sure your children understand that they can feel and express respect not only for individuals, but also beyond that for entire cultures.

So once a week during Respect for Others Month, expose your children to cultures other than your own. That doesn't mean this is the only time you should make that effort, but during this month, make it a conscious priority. It can be anything from travel to another country (nice, if you can manage it!) to reading a book, or watching a video.

My family happens to live in a large metropolitan area, so for this exercise, we might take the kids to a play based on an Arab folktale or walk around Chinatown to explore the shops and restaurants. In our experience with our children, ethnic food is a great bridge into another culture. They may not be willing to try the most exotic things on the menu, but it is fun to expose them to the different types of food.

You don't need to live near a city to do this exercise. Even listening to a CD of folktales from around the world while in the car is a start. That's what we did while I shuttled my kids to and from my son's piano lessons. The one we like is *Tales of Wisdom and Wonder*. We still listen to that CD even though my kids have pretty much memorized the whole thing. They are fascinated with things that are different from their everyday lives. They love the idea that kids in other countries grow up listening to these stories and they get a chance to hear them too. It's easy to find CDs like this on the Internet or at your local bookstore or library.

The whole point of this exercise is to familiarize children with the beauty and richness found in *all* cultural traditions. Ignorance is often a breeding ground for disrespect and even hate, not only in our society, but throughout the world as well. On the other hand, knowledge fosters understanding, so by getting your children out of their cultural comfort zones, they can experience something completely new to them that will truly broaden their horizons. And experiencing another culture doesn't have to be a different ethnicity. Exploring a different "culture" could be visiting with children or adults with

Month Three

significant physical or intellectual disabilities, or spending time with people who practice a different organized religion than your family. Too often, with our hectic schedules, we allow the lives of our children to become very narrow and routine. This exercise helps change that.

Believe me, it doesn't have to be a big production. None of these exercises are meant to strain your already busy schedule, or your wallet for that matter. This is meant to open the door to different experiences so your children can be more aware and appreciative of other nationalities, races, and religions. For one thing, many families are already multicultural, mine included. So, many of us are already *embracing*—not *tolerating*—a culture that is different from what we grew up knowing. How lucky are we?

Variations on Expand Your Horizons

Try any of these or come up with your own ideas for cultural experiences your family will enjoy.

Kids love to play games, so have fun while expanding their cultural horizons. You can try a board game called "Passport to Culture" that has all kinds of interesting facts about different cultures in the world, or just play a game from another culture! You can look up games online and start playing them with things you have around the house or in your yard. You can even try board games like Mahjong from China.

With your children, learn to say "hello," thank you," and "goodbye" in different languages. If this inspires you, go beyond that and sign your kids and yourself up for classes to learn a foreign language. *Bonne chance!*

Invite a friend or family member from a different culture over for dinner and ask them to share a treasured recipe from their country that you can all make together.

If you live in or near a city, spend the day in Greek Town, Little Italy, Chinatown, . . . and so on, with your family.

Music is a great way to experience another culture. Listen to an ethnic station on the radio, or to world music on National Public Radio, or download some ethnic tunes on your phone and dance around the living room with your kids!

Learn to play an instrument from another culture.

Arrange a visit to a nursing home so your kids have an opportunity to interact with and show respect to their elders if they don't have grandparents nearby.

Go to the library and borrow books about other cultures.

Rent a family movie set in another country, even if it has subtitles. Especially if it has subtitles!

Go to local ethnic art fairs and look for paintings or drawings representing other cultures. Display your favorites in your home.

Search for websites about different cultures. Visit the sites on your own first and when you find ones you like, have your children join you to explore the sites.

One-Time Exercise: Family Rules of Respect

At the end of this month, have your family look back at the time you have spent focusing on respect. Ask your children to help you come up with the ten most important ways they feel your family can show respect to each other, and to people outside the immediate family. These are the "Family Rules of Respect" and they should reflect participation and input from the children as well as the adults. This will not only provide an opportunity for you to show respect to your children by including them in an important decision, but in my experience it will also make it more likely that they will follow the rules because they are invested in them. Use the respect tiles as a starting point. It's important that your kids know you want them to be respectful of others, but also, they should understand that they too are deserving of respect and dignity. So while you're coming up with your list, stress that each rule of respect that your family decides on in this exercise is meant to be reciprocal. If my son points out that we should include "Knock before entering," or my daughter wants to include "Don't interrupt," then they should strive to follow those rules. But also, my son should expect that the rest of us will be knocking on his door rather than barging in, and my daughter should know that we will consistently wait until she is finished with what she is saying before we speak.

Post the rules of respect in your kitchen so you all see them every day.

The point of this exercise is to home in on the rules you all feel would best represent your intention as a family to live respectfully. Below I've listed the rules our family has posted.

Our Family Rules of Respect:

1. Obey your parents
2. Tell the truth
3. Tidy up after yourself
4. Knock before entering
5. Ask permission before borrowing something
6. Don't judge others
7. Treat each other's property carefully
8. Use good hygiene
9. Don't interrupt
10. Use good manners

Variations on Family Rules of Respect:

Make it more personal for your family by using your last name, such as the "Martinez Rules of Respect." That reminds everyone in your family that you all agreed to these rules. They are the guiding principles of respect specifically for your family. You can also create artwork or take pictures of your kids with each "rule" you choose. For example: "Don't stare," "Be on time," or "Be a good sport," and have your local drugstore make them into mugs, magnets for your fridge, key chains, custom stamps, note pads—you name it. You can do this using an online service as well. Just do a search for "photo gifts." If you and your family use the computer a lot, you can make your "rules" into your screensaver where you'll see them every day.

Staying Power

Long after Respect for Others Month, I was reading in the master bedroom when all of a sudden my son unexpectedly walked in. I looked up, surprised, and he stood there for a moment, about to say something. Just then, he stopped himself, turned around and walked out of the room, closing the door quietly behind him. It was great to see him figuring it out for himself. A few seconds later, I heard a knock at the door. "Mom, may I come in?" he said. All that without my saying a word.

And the best thing is that now my children don't look at respect as a vague, abstract concept anymore. It's real to them and it has a place in their everyday lives. All around my house, long after Respect for Others Month is over, my kids are knocking on doors, asking to borrow things (more often than not), using good manners—and then some.

In order to keep the lessons of respect going with your family, continue to use the respect tiles as coasters to remind everyone in the family of the many ways to show respect. If you didn't make the tiles, simply encourage and reinforce respectful behavior when you see it. Also, point it out when you see someone in the family being disrespectful. Remind your kids to tell others when they have crossed the line into disrespect. And the next time you go to the library or bookstore, or even out to eat, consider it an opportunity to bring other cultures into your lives. Make an effort to expose your kids to new cultural experiences that will foster respect for other people.

Experiencing Respect for Others Month with your family can be eye opening. You may have found that you were insisting that your children respect other adults, like teachers and coaches, yet you didn't expect the same respectful treatment from them yourself. Or, you may have realized that the way you spoke to your children wasn't always as respectful as it should have been. Now that you have your "Family Rules of Respect" posted where your whole family can see it every day, it should be a gentle, yet constant, reminder of how everyone in the family should treat each other—kids and parents alike.

Month Four

INTEGRITY

Doing what's right for the right reasons

Integrity is one of the most important values I can think of, and it seems to be getting more and more difficult to find. Many people seem to think integrity is just plain old-fashioned. Maybe it is. But it shouldn't be. As you spend this month teaching your children about the importance of integrity, once again you have an opportunity to go deeper with a value. You can teach your children to go beyond honesty, to being an ethical person with integrity. This month you can show your children that telling the truth is good, but living the truth is better.

Truth is very important to me. That's why I must stop right here and tell you about something that happened recently. I caught Grace stealing again. Once more, my sugar-craving daughter was led astray by candy. I had recently opened a bag of lollypops to give her a special treat. Organic, naturally sweetened lollypops, mind you. Foolishly, I left the bag on the dresser in the master bedroom. Only about ten days had passed when I picked up the bag, so I expected it to be fairly heavy. After all, there would be close to the original sixty lollypops in the bag, wouldn't there? Not so much. There were maybe twenty lollypops. My daughter had polished off forty lollypops in the scope of a week and a half!

So, as I was driving home with Grace after this discovery, I brought up the issue of stealing. She explained her dilemma rather eloquently.

"Mom, here's the problem. It's like there are two parts of me. One part wants to do the right thing and walk away from the candy, but the other part of me wants the candy so bad. And that part of me is much stronger so I can't stop myself!"

I'm touched by her admission that she struggled with this a bit. At least a part of her knows that stealing is wrong. Now we just have to help make that part of her stronger so she makes the right decision in the future.

I asked Grace a question. "Are you an honest person or a dishonest person?"

"An honest person," she replied quietly.

"Would an honest person steal forty lollypops?" I asked.

"Nope," she replied, even quieter now.

"So, are you an honest person?" I asked again.

My daughter didn't answer me out loud, but as I looked in the rear view mirror, I could see her faintly shake her head "no."

"But I want to be, Mommy" she said, her voice sounding stronger now.

"Well then, kiddo, you can't steal. An honest person doesn't steal. If you want to be an honest person, then when you feel tempted to steal candy or anything else, come to Daddy or me and ask for help. Or if you're at school, somewhere we can't help you at that moment, say a little prayer and ask God to help you be an honest person."

You may be asking yourself, if this system of teaching values really works, why is my daughter stealing candy after she's gone through Integrity Month? But that's exactly why I had to tell you. If I have integrity then I have to let you know that this system, like any other, is not perfect. And no one in my family—or any family—is perfect. However, this system isn't about striving for perfection. Not even close. It's about doing your best to teach your values to your kids in some small but significant way, every day.

As you go through this year of values with your kids, keep in mind that some things will really stay with them and stick in their psyches and their hearts. And some things won't, at least not right away or not completely. And something that really makes a lasting impression on your ten year old may not make much of a dent with your five year old. Frankly, each child is different and may need more help with certain values than others do.

Know Who You Are

During Integrity Month, I often say to my children, "Know who you are." If self-respect is the foundation upon which their lives are built, integrity is the cornerstone. It's something they can go back to again and again to remind themselves of who they are. If a child is in a situation where they can tell a lie or tell the truth, then each time it's like they are deciding in that individual situation to lie or tell the truth. It could go either way depending on various factors. Will they get in trouble if they admit the truth? Can they actually get away with it if they lie? But if children have that cornerstone of knowing who they are and if they are secure in their own integrity, then they don't really have to deal with the dilemma on a case-by-case basis, sometimes lying and sometimes telling the truth. They know who they are, and that knowledge does not allow them to both lie and stay true to who they are, so they learn to tell the truth. Even if it has consequences.

Before we had this month-by-month system of teaching values to our children, my husband and I realized that all the times we had insisted that our kids "tell the truth," we had simply been teaching them *not to tell lies*. A good thing for sure, but we were woefully treading the surface of what being honest really means. One of the goals of Integrity Month is for children to think about what kind of people they are now and who they want to be as they grow up and become adults. In my experience, the question I asked my daughter, "Are you an honest person?" is more powerful than asking "Is it wrong to tell a lie?" That's because integrity goes beyond just being honest.

Integrity isn't just telling the truth, though that is a good start. Integrity is about being ethical, being able to declare your beliefs and stand up for them, even when no one else is backing you up. It's also about making sacrifices for others, and doing the right thing, even when it's hard. Because, let's face it, living a life of integrity isn't always easy. As my husband has said, "Integrity is sometimes about choosing the path less traveled because you believe it's the right thing to do regardless of what other people may think."

It can be quite difficult for children to understand integrity in a concrete way. So during this month, look for ways to make this value real to your children. There are so many small but very significant ways to show kids how to do the right thing. To start, you may want to consciously point out examples of how you and your spouse or partner, or other people in their lives such as teachers, grandparents, aunts, and uncles are making choices that show integrity. Focus on actions that show simple honesty, since that is the building block for integrity. At the grocery store when you are given too much change, point it out to your children and let them see you return the money to the lady at the checkout counter. As you leave the store, ask them if they think you did the right thing and if so, why? Or when the waiter at a restaurant mistakenly doesn't charge you for the dessert you enjoyed, ask your kids, "What should we do here? How can we make a choice that shows we are people of integrity?"

Sometimes, however, kids don't absorb lessons from everyday life as well as they do from things like movies, TV shows, and electronic games. My kids love all those things, especially movies, so during this month, I consciously choose to watch movies with my kids that demonstrate integrity.

One of their favorites is *Charlie and The Chocolate Factory* where Charlie shows integrity while the other kids scheme and whine to get their way. Charlie's decency wins him the chance to inherit the glorious chocolate factory. I talked to my son about this, and as he pointed out to me, that's the moment in the film when Charlie's integrity truly shines through. When Charlie, who has lived a life of poverty and hunger, has to make a difficult choice between going home to his family with nothing or accepting the chocolate factory but never seeing his family again, he makes a choice based on integrity. He sacrifices the sweet, bountiful, and adventurous life with Mr. Wonka and the chocolate factory and chooses instead to stay with his family whom he loves more than anything. Ultimately, that decision saves him and his entire family from poverty.

But having integrity isn't about rewards. It's about doing what's right *because it's right.* The inner peace that comes with having integrity is its own reward. One way to explain this concept to children is to talk to them about when they have lied or withheld the truth, or taken something that didn't belong to them. Ask them how they felt before the truth came out. Did they feel uncomfortable in any way? Did it bother them when they thought about what they had done or did they worry about being caught? Their conscience is the part of them deep down inside that knows right from wrong, and wants them to choose what is right. If they don't, that part of them just doesn't quite feel well. They might just feel uneasy, and they might spend a lot of time thinking about what they did—or in some cases what they should have done, but didn't. And sometimes they might even have physical symptoms like tummy aches or headaches. Feeling guilty is no fun. So talk to your kids about how listening to their consciences can help them do the right thing and avoid all that uneasiness and guilt.

Supplies for This Month's Exercises

- Index cards or small pieces of paper for the daily and weekly exercises
- Your computer to print out questions for the daily exercise (if you'd like)
- A glass jar or bowl to hold your index cards
- At the end of the month, you'll need a few raw eggs!

Daily Exercise: Daily Dilemmas

The exercises for this month will give kids clear-cut, tangible examples of how they can live their lives with honesty and integrity. They provide great starting points for how integrity can be a very real part of their everyday lives.

On the first day of Integrity Month, sit down with your spouse or partner and come up with thirty daily moral dilemmas that your children might face in their lives. On index cards, write down a question starting with the words "What would you do if . . . " for each day of the month. You might write things like, "What would you do if a classmate offered to share the correct answers to an upcoming math test with you and you hadn't studied?" Or, "What would you do if you were at the movies seeing a brand new film with your friends and one of them started taping it with a video camera he had hidden under his coat?" Or, "What would you do if you bought lunch at school and were given too much change when you paid?" Try to give your children many opportunities to think about situations that might actually happen to them in their day-to-day lives when they have to choose between being dishonest or living with integrity.

Place the index cards in a large bowl or cookie jar and every day during this month, pull out a card and ask each of your kids to answer the question on that day's card. After you ask each child the question and hear his or her answers, ask "And what do you think was the right thing to do in that situation?" Of course, the answer they choose and what we feel is the "right thing to do" is sometimes different. Ask them, "How would you feel after you made your choice? Would you feel proud of yourself? Would you feel uncomfortable or guilty?" Encourage them to consider those questions whenever they are faced with a moral dilemma, no matter how small. Also, let them know how you would answer each question. You can do this exercise during breakfast, while you're walking your kids to school, or as you sit at the table after dinner each night. Pick a time that is part of your daily routine and it won't feel like something extra to do in your already busy day.

Often, moral dilemmas can be heightened in the presence of peer pressure, which can make kids feel unsure about doing the right thing. Cara, a mom who spent a month focusing on integrity with her husband Mark and their three daughters, ages three, five, and ten, talked about that issue with her ten-year-old daughter. One day, the Daily Dilemma for their daughter was what she would do if she saw someone stealing from a classmate's backpack at school. Her daughter responded thoughtfully that she would tell the person who owned the backpack about it and then would tell an adult. Cara found this was a great way to start the discussion about choosing to do the right thing over doing what would make her daughter popular.

What has been interesting with my kids is that they often try to see if there is room for ethical compromise. One day, the question my kids pulled out of the bowl was "What would you do if you were having a really great time at a neighborhood carnival and earned enough points to actually win a prize? But the prize you were given was much better than what you qualified for, and it was something you really wanted?" (The questions are not always this long or elaborate, but I like to paint a picture for my kids so they can really imagine themselves in the situation.) My daughter said she would tell the person running the game that she had been given the wrong prize. My son's answer was a little more complex. He said he would take the prize because he had "earned it." When I pointed out that in fact, he had not earned that particular prize, he still said he would take it. Seeing a good opportunity for a learning moment, I took out a piece of paper and drew a little diagram with two rectangles on either side of the paper. I colored one box in and left the other one as is. I shaded the area in between the two little rectangles and told them that the area in the middle is a sort of "gray area." I explained that the gray area is the place between doing the absolute wrong thing and doing the absolute right thing. And of course, sometimes it can be a bit confusing to know if something is absolutely right or wrong. But sometimes people use that gray area to justify their actions, even when they know in their hearts that they are not doing the right thing.

I pointed out to my son that he was trying to justify taking the better prize by going to that gray area. I told him that although it hadn't been his fault that he received a better prize than he had earned, it was his responsibility, if he wants to be a person of integrity, to point out the error. My daughter was still sitting there with us, so I posed a question to both of them.

"Do you think it hurts anyone when you walk away with a better prize at a carnival, or when the woman at the checkout gives me an extra $10 in change and I keep it? In other words, does it hurt anyone else if we are dishonest, or don't show integrity?"

Neither of them thought it did, but I pointed out that even a small thing we do, or don't do, can have a big impact on someone else. For instance, the man at the carnival might get in trouble with his boss for giving out the more valuable prize. The woman at the checkout counter might have to make up the difference out of her own pocket when she tallies up her cash register and her receipts at the end of the day. And what if this has happened to her before? Might she even lose her job? How will she pay her bills?

Kids don't always consider that there are often ripple effects based on the decisions we make in our lives. Making unethical and dishonest decisions, even ones that seem insignificant, like taking that prize at the carnival or walking away with an extra $10 at the grocery store, can hurt other people. And even though we may never know how, or if, our actions have hurt someone else, it is still something we should take into consideration.

Use a moment like this to point out to your kids that we shouldn't do what we believe is the "right" thing because we think we will get rewarded or avoid doing the "wrong" thing just because it might possibly hurt someone, though, of course, that is something we don't want to happen. We should do our best to try to do the "right" thing *because* it's right, not because of any perceived reward or potential punishment.

With this exercise, you may find that you can use the same question for both kids even if there is an age difference. Interestingly enough, I find that things often appear much more "black and white" to my daughter, while my son, who is five years older, often finds himself in that gray area. Or, it might be best to have different questions based on your child's age or maturity level. Here are some questions we've used for this exercise:

What Would You Do If . . .

- You broke a toy, or damaged a video game that a friend had loaned to you and you have to return it today?
- You received your graded test back from the teacher and you realize she mistakenly gave you a higher grade than you had earned, but you need that grade to qualify for the baseball team and you are one of the school's best players?
- You spilled juice on your grandmother's new couch when you had been told not to bring any food or drinks into her living room?
- You saw your best friend steal something from the teacher's desk?
- The school bully's favorite target falls asleep on the bus ride home after school and is about to miss his stop? Do you wake him and risk the bully turning his attention toward you?
- You hadn't studied for the math test at school. Should you fake being sick or go to school and risk failing the test?

- A nice but unpopular girl in your class invites you to her birthday party. Do you go and risk the popular kids excluding you from their parties or do you lie and make up an excuse to avoid going?

- You notice a $20 bill fall out of your babysitter's pocket on the very same day that a new DVD is coming out—and it has bonus features!

- Your parents ask if you've finished your homework and you haven't, but your friend is coming over any minute with his new video game?

- It's time to return the movie you rented from the video store but your dad can't find it because you were really careless with it and you scratched the DVD?

- Your little sister was really hungry and she was looking in the fridge for the last nectarine but you had just grabbed it and were about to eat it yourself?

- The new video game your uncle gave you for your birthday is really fun but it has some violence—something your mom would never allow—but she's not home from work yet so she might not find out?

- The popular kids at school decide to play a mean prank on the new teacher and they ask you to be a part of it?

- A new movie you really want to see is premiering on TV tonight but you're grounded from watching television all week. Your grandma is babysitting and doesn't seem to know you shouldn't watch TV . . . ?

- Your teacher praises you for a great idea in a project you did with a classmate who is not at school that day. The idea wasn't yours—it was your classmate's. Do you take the credit or let the teacher know it wasn't your idea?

- You are goofing around with your friends leaving school one day and you accidentally brush up against your principal's car and scratch the paint?
- You jokingly make a comment that a classmate thinks is true and then she spreads it as a rumor. Do you admit how it got started?

Be sure to provide an environment for your children to talk about these dilemmas honestly so they can give answers that are real, rather than just saying what you want to hear. Remind them that this is Integrity Month and therefore you are really trying to find out where they are on these issues. This isn't about judging them. It's a way to learn more about your children and to get a better understanding of the moral and ethical situations they find themselves in every day. It's also a great opportunity to teach and guide them.

Variations on Daily Dilemmas:

Instead of the parents coming up with the dilemmas, you might ask your children for instances when they have felt torn and unsure about what to do when faced with a difficult ethical choice. Or, if you know of particular situations your child has faced recently, you can use these as the basis for a moral dilemma. What choices did your child make and what were the repercussions? Or you can share stories with them about moral dilemmas faced by you or other family members or even historical figures like George Washington (and his cherry tree) or contemporary celebrities or sports figures.

Weekly Exercise: Giving a Promise

One night a week during this month, your family should sit down and each make a specific, short-term promise to someone else in the family—or you could make a promise to yourselves. This promise is meant to be kept during that week. Write the promise on a piece of paper and give it to the person to whom you have promised something. When someone is making a promise to themselves, for example, "I promise to introduce myself to all the kids in summer camp this week even though I'm shy," tape it up on the bedroom wall or someplace they'll see it. It serves as a great reminder during the week.

Your son might promise to teach his sister how to play a simple song on the piano, and your daughter could promise to help you clean out your closet so you can give clothes to charity. Maybe your partner could promise you that he or she will make your favorite dish for dinner that week or you might promise you'll clean out the "junk drawer" in the kitchen. Again, everyone will have one week to keep his or her particular promise. At the end of the week, gather again as a family and see which promises were kept and which ones were not. Whoever doesn't keep his or her promise can simply throw away the piece of paper. When that happens, there is no need for anyone to apologize or feel guilty. This exercise is designed to let everyone in the family, especially the kids, see how they feel when they disregard or honor a promise. There are no external consequences or rewards. When a promise has been honored, the piece of paper with that promise is placed in a glass jar, but not as a reward. It's just nice to hold on to those "kept" promises and see them add up as the month goes on. Each week your family has a chance to make new promises.

This way, especially if a child is feeling a little down about not keeping a promise, he or she has the chance to try again.

Variations on Giving a Promise:

You might make the exercise a bit more challenging and write the names of all the family members on different pieces of paper. Have everyone pick a name out of a hat or a bowl; each person has to make a promise to the person whose name they picked. As the weeks go on, you could start making promises to people outside your immediate family by adding "teacher" or "grandparent" to the list— even "friend," or "co-worker" for the grownups. I often tell my kids' teachers and grandparents what value we are working on because we like to see our family's experience of the particular value spread beyond the four of us.

One-Time Exercise: Where's the Trust?

Since Integrity Month is all about being honest, this is a great time to bring up Aesop's fable "The Boy Who Cried Wolf."

The first time we talked about this story I asked my children, "What very valuable thing did the little boy have at the beginning of the story that he didn't have at the end?"

Inevitably they said, "Sheep!" Well, that's true enough, but that wasn't what I was going for. At the beginning of the story, the little boy had something even more valuable than the sheep. It was so valuable in fact, that it could have protected the sheep from the wolf. In a word, he had trust. The villagers trusted him and treated him as a person with integrity. After all, who would be foolhardy enough to joke about a dangerous thing like a wolf? Who would mock their collective efforts to save the precious sheep? The little boy—that's who. Once the villagers realized that this little boy lacked integrity, they stopped giving him their trust, and without it, he and the poor sheep were quite lost.

The goal of this one-time exercise is to help your children understand that integrity is priceless and is not to be squandered. This is a very serious thought, and you may find that children sometimes get overwhelmed learning about values when things get too serious. So it's time to have some fun and play a game!

The game, Where's The Trust? draws on the concepts of trusting someone and being trusted.

Each family member should sit in a circle on the kitchen floor, with every other person holding a raw egg in his or her hands—if there are an even number of people in your family. If not, use one egg for three people, two eggs for five people, and so on. With eyes closed, or blindfolded, each person with an egg should pass it to the person on his or her left. You can talk if you want to, giving verbal cues as you go. Start out slowly and then as you learn to trust each other more, pick up speed. Additionally, after you have made it around the circle two times, everyone should move a bit further away from each other.

You may find that things get pretty silly because no sooner have you carefully placed an egg into someone's hands than someone else is gingerly handing you their egg. You may even like to play fast music in the background to keep the game moving. The initial idea behind the game was that as soon as the egg(s)—and the trust—got broken, we would stop the game and clean up the mess. But a funny thing happened when my family played this game. The eggs didn't break. And as we passed them from person to person, an interesting thing occurred quite organically. My daughter started saying, "I trust you," as she passed the egg. So we each started saying it. That wasn't part of the game. It just happened. And I realized that the point of the exercise was not that the trust would be broken, but that the trust was *there* already.

This game can also be played at the kitchen table, but you may find it's more fun (and easier to clean) if you sit on the kitchen floor. And I say easier to clean because although the eggs did not break during the game, our children begged us to let them play catch with the eggs afterward. They couldn't resist throwing them and seeing them break, and we couldn't blame them! And although we have talked to our kids about trust before in their lives, I suspect that when years have gone by, they may not remember all those conversations. But I know they will remember the night of breaking eggs and finding trust.

Variations on Where's the Trust?

Weather permitting, you can do this exercise outside with water balloons. Or you could try another (less messy) game to show the importance of trusting and being trusted. An obstacle course—with participants blindfolded—is a fun way to explore trust. Games like these are often used to build trust in corporations or even in improvisational comedy classes. One person guides the blindfolded person who obviously is unable to see what he or she is doing. Various silly objects are placed on the floor or ground and the person who is guiding does their best to navigate the course for their teammate. Safety is key here, so make sure there are no hard objects or furniture to bump into. Ideally, have the children be the ones leading the parents through the obstacle course so they can have the experience of being trusted by a grownup.

Staying Power

Since spending a month focusing on integrity, my kids have demonstrated a deeper appreciation for the truth. They now have a sense of why it is important to live their lives with honesty and integrity. Recently, when I told my son not to play his video games for longer than twenty minutes unless he had first gotten permission, he actually declared his promise aloud. "I, Connor, promise not to play the game past twenty minutes unless given permission." I was impressed then, but even more so a week later when he had an opportunity to continue to play the video game while I was doing something else and wouldn't necessarily have known. He came to me and told me that he had been tempted to keep playing the game but talked himself out of it and decided to come to me instead. Incidentally, when he did that, I praised him for his integrity but did not reward him with more time playing the game. And he didn't ask for more time either. Knowing he had made the right choice was reward in itself.

And I'm delighted to report that as Grace and I recently waited at the counter in a card store, she eyed the rows of delicious candy and walked away from temptation. She told me that she just couldn't take the candy because she's an honest person, and an honest person doesn't steal.

There are many ways to keep the lessons of Integrity Month ongoing in your family's lives. For one thing, when you make promises to your partner or children, keep them! Acknowledge how much it means to you when your partner or child gives you a promise and honors it. Trust is very important within a family. And because you've explored many moral dilemmas with your children this month, let them know you will continue to talk to them about the issues they face.

But even after spending this month teaching your kids about the importance of integrity, you may still catch them in a lie sometimes. That happens. Old habits are hard to break and many kids are just used to saying what they think their parents and teachers want to hear. After all, when they have told the truth in the past, it has sometimes gotten them in trouble. So the important thing is getting kids to understand that if they want to be an honest person—if they see themselves that way—then they must tell the truth.

As a parent, you can reinforce this by not overreacting when they do tell you that truth, whatever it is. "Yes, Mom, I cheated on the test." Or "Yeah, Dad, it was me who took the comic books from my brother's room." After spending this month focusing on integrity with them, realize that by telling you the truth, even if they did a bad thing, they are making progress! Of course, you have to address the "bad thing"— you're a parent and that's your job. But if you can, start out by first letting your son or daughter know that you are proud of them for telling the truth and that it was the right thing to do. That's a good starting point that you can build on long after this month is over.

Month Five

COMPASSION

The inspiration for kindness

Maybe your kids see you do compassionate things all the time. You watch out for an elderly neighbor, give blood at the local twice-yearly drive in your community, and are the first one to lend a hand when a friend is sick and in need of help. Or maybe that's not you at all. You're so busy just trying to keep things together—raising kids and working full-time, not to mention your dog just had six puppies. You're a good person, but you don't have time to even think about being compassionate, let alone teach it to your kids.

No matter where you see yourself in these scenarios, if you want to raise compassionate children who care about other people and do something about it, then you will get a lot out of this chapter. Compassion doesn't have to take a lot of time—it can be expressed in a kind word or a gentle smile. But even if your kids see you being kind, does that mean they will absorb that quality automatically? It depends on the child, but generally kids need more than that in my experience. To help your children grow up to be caring and compassionate human beings, take this month to focus on this quiet but extremely powerful value with your kids. It may make all the difference—not just to your kids, but to the people who will be touched by their kindness.

Compassion in Action

Back when my husband and I originally decided to take a month to teach our children the importance of this value, we debated a bit—should we focus on compassion or kindness? Are they the same thing? My son helped clarify this when he asked me what compassion actually is. I told him that compassion is being aware that someone else is suffering and wanting to do something to ease their pain. And I believe the act of doing something to help someone who is hurting is kindness. In other words, kindness is compassion in action.

"Remember that time when I had just come home from my friend's funeral?" I asked my son. "I was sitting in the kitchen just staring into space, and without saying a word you put a hot cup of tea on the counter in front of me. You noticed that I was suffering and wanted to ease my pain—that's compassion.

Then you did something about it and gave me something comforting—that's kindness."

Showing your children the connection between compassion and kindness is important because your goal with every value you teach your children is to look for the deeper meaning. Because Compassion Month comes after you have taught your children about gratitude, self-respect, respect for others, and integrity, you can build on what they have learned in those previous months. Because they have focused on gratitude and have started being people who have a deep appreciation for the blessings in their lives, they have an awareness of all the times others have shown kindness to them. Having a stronger sense of who they are after Self-Respect Month allows them to show compassion in a situation where it might not be the coolest thing to do in the eyes of other kids their age. When your daughter asks a kid that the other students think of as nerdy to eat lunch with her, it may not win any approval from the clique of ultracool kids, but if she respects herself, she can have the courage to be kind to a kid who is feeling lonely and isolated. And reaching out to someone in need in a way that preserves their dignity and honors their humanity comes from respecting others. Since you have focused on integrity with your kids, they know their actions should to be true to themselves, and genuine. Just like you taught your children during Gratitude Month, that there should be a "match" between being grateful and saying thank you, kids should also understand that there is a connection between feeling empathy for someone and doing something to ease their suffering. Because clearly it is possible to feel compassion for someone else, and want to help, yet end up doing nothing. Also, there are times when an individual, a group, or even a whole corporation does something for others that outwardly seems kind, but is actually motivated by something other than compassion. Perhaps the "giver" has the need for attention, wants to be liked or respected, or simply hopes to appear altruistic. That's not really kindness. And we're going for the real thing here.

So during this month, encourage your children to see compassion and kindness as partners. The goal is to show them the significance of acts of kindness rooted in genuine compassion. In short, you want your children to feel empathy and then do something about it.

It is easy for children to become overwhelmed when you discuss the importance of living their lives with compassion and kindness. After all, these concepts can be intimidating. There's a tendency to think that in order to make a difference, you have to do something big. Surely something small won't matter. Why donate $5 to help after a hurricane if millions of dollars are needed? Why make dinner for a terminally ill friend if it won't save her? Why say a kind word to a stranger you'll never see again? Quite simply, it matters. These small acts of kindness have an effect, though they may not seem apparent at the time.

During Compassion Month, do your best to impress upon your children that *any* act of kindness, no matter how small it may seem, is truly powerful. A simple word of empathy or a kind gesture can have a profound and lasting impact, not only on the person who receives it, but also on the person who is being kind. Compassion makes us powerful. Anyone, even a small child, can be powerful when he or she is kind. And there is a never-ending supply of compassion at our feet and in our hearts just waiting to be put into action. As my son said to me, "Sometimes the small good thing you do today has a big effect for years." I love that idea and I love that he feels that way. Kindness has a ripple effect.

Oftentimes you'll never know the power of your kind act in the world, but it's out there, doing good. Think about it. If we suddenly had the power to turn all the meanness and cruelty in the world into compassion and kindness, can you even imagine the outcome? Certainly there would be less anger, less crime, and less war. At a more personal level, there would be less anguish, less insecurity and less isolation. And there would be more gentleness, more peace. The impact would be profound.

What You'll Need for the Daily Exercise:

- A calendar printed from the Internet
- A dry erase board could also be used, or the kids could create their own calendar on construction paper or on poster board, leaving room to write something on each date.

The other exercises for this month don't require supplies.

Daily Exercise: Compassion in Action Calendar

My husband and I have been blessed with amazing examples of the power of compassion in our mothers, who are both extraordinarily caring people. In many ways, compassion has become one of those values that many people think just comes out for special occasions, like when there is a natural disaster or when someone close to you loses a loved one. But that's not what our mothers taught us and that's not the goal of Compassion Month. Compassion is an everyday value, something we want our children to take with them, so to speak, everywhere they go. So the first exercise for this month is designed to show children the impact of doing one small kind act in a compassionate way every day.

At the beginning of this month, sit down with your family and talk about concrete ways you can show compassion to other people. Print out a calendar of that month and write down one idea on each date. One day might be "notice people." Just that. On that day, ask your kids to make a special effort to be aware of the people they encounter. Does the teacher seem tired? Does your son's classmate look frustrated or overwhelmed with their schoolwork? Is your daughter's friend at gymnastics just not acting like herself? Interestingly enough, just noticing others seems to foster kindness and your children may come home with stories of things they have done throughout their day that went beyond just "noticing." If your kids are aware of how others around them are feeling, it can spur them into action. Your son might ask the teacher if he can do something to help out after school or your daughter might offer to share her snack with her fellow gymnast.

This can really be eye opening for grownups too. Many of us just seem to be on autopilot, rushing through our days without even noticing the people we encounter—at times, even our own families. Taking a moment to be more aware of the people we interact with can help us notice if they are sad, stressed, or just plain overwhelmed, and that gives us the opportunity to feel compassion and see if there is anything we can do to help.

Karen and her husband Bill experienced Compassion Month with their four children—daughters ages nine, eight and five, and a six-year-old son. One day, the directive on their Compassion in Action Calendar was simply "to be friendly." Their nine-year-old daughter took the opportunity to show around a new classmate and ate lunch with her as well. Their six-year-old son helped a classmate who was running late pack up his lunch. On the day the calendar read "Pay someone a compliment," their five-year-old daughter felt really good when she pointed out to a friend how much she liked her headband, which made her friend smile. And their eight-year-old daughter complimented a friend's coat and said it made her feel happy just by doing that. Karen knew her kids were wonderful people, but she found that compassion came much more naturally to her children than she had ever realized. Focusing on this value with her children made it easy for them to express kindness every day.

In our family, every evening during this month we have a little chat about how we each put compassion into action that day. I put aside a plastic bag full of loose change and each time someone in our family does something kind, born of genuine compassion, we take one of the coins and put it in a jar in the kitchen. If you choose to do this, you can use pennies, nickels, dimes, quarters or even dollars if you can manage it. My kids really respond well to visual aides. They love seeing the coins pile up as the month goes on. At the end of the month, we have a calendar filled with acts of kindness and a jar full of loose change. We take the money we've collected all month and donate it to charity.

Here are other ways to show compassion. Many of the ideas below are geared toward the kids, but everyone in the family should participate.

- Make a snack for someone in your family.
- Say something kind to someone today.
- Give someone a genuine compliment today.
- Find something that you don't use anymore, like shoes or clothes that don't fit, or books or toys you have outgrown, and collect them to donate to a charity.
- Help someone at home, school, or work today.
- Send a handwritten letter to a relative who doesn't hear from you often enough.
- Make someone feel welcome.
- Use a kind tone of voice today even when (especially when) you feel like being mean or sarcastic.
- Notice the kindness you receive from others today rather than taking it for granted.
- Say hello to someone at school (or work) today that you don't usually talk to.
- Help an animal today. If you don't have a pet, you could put out birdseed in a birdfeeder or recycle your garbage at home to make the planet a better place for wild animals to live. Everything matters!
- Share something today.
- Be friendly.
- Make a conscious effort to accept people as they are without judgment.
- Hold a door for someone today, or say "After you" when entering a room with someone else.

- Each member of the family should call a loved one today just to say hi and check in with him or her.
- Today, ask how someone is doing and then really listen to any problems that person may have without bringing up your own issues.
- When someone makes a mistake today, don't criticize—instead take the opportunity to encourage him or her.
- Offer to let someone go in front of you in line at the school cafeteria, at the grocery store, in traffic, or anywhere you are waiting today.
- Make a conscious effort to smile at people today!
- Give someone a gift from your heart—maybe a hand-made card, a small bouquet of flowers, or an apple for your teacher.
- When you know someone is suffering in some way, say a prayer for him or her, or if you don't feel comfortable doing that, simply wish the person well in your heart.
- Offer to help a family member with a chore he or she normally does alone.

Be sure to do these acts of kindness along with your children and share what you have done with them every evening. You never want your kids to think that these values are just for them—they should know that you strive to live these values every day in your adult lives. And by sharing your experiences with showing compassion in your everyday lives, they can see specific ways they can be kind as they become adults.

Instead of making a calendar, you could have each member of the family decide a good way to show kindness each day. So one day, everyone in the family uses Mom's suggestion. The next day, it's one of the kids' turn to choose the way each member of the family can show compassion in action. For the more crafty among you, especially if you have younger kids, make a compassion version of an "Advent Calendar" where you have two layers of cardstock paper. The inside layer has each act of kindness like "Hug someone in your family" and the second layer of paper has a small "door" that matches up to the comment underneath. Every morning, the kids open one of the doors and behind it is the way they can show kindness that day.

Weekly Exercise: Switching Places

Children are sometimes very focused on themselves, and they can have difficulty understanding the suffering of others. How many times have you seen your child do something thoughtless or hurtful and then said to him or her, "How would you feel if that happened to you?" The goal of the weekly exercise this month is to give your kids the opportunity to put themselves in someone else's place and try to experience that person's feelings.

During this role-playing exercise, ask your kids to "switch places" with someone they know—or might not know at all. Perhaps they pretend to be an elderly woman on a bus, looking for a seat. Or they role-play as a new kid in school who doesn't know anyone and feels self-conscious and alone on

Month Five

the playground at recess. Ask the kids to tell you how they feel as that person. If you have more than one child, one of them can role-play as the person in need of compassion and the other child can play the person who is moved to perform an act of kindness. Or, if you only have one child, a parent can join in. As you do this exercise each week, make sure the children get the chance to role-play as a person who needs compassion and one who offers it. Each week, use a different scenario and let each child role-play in a situation that is age appropriate, and is something they may encounter in their daily lives.

Here are some other examples that work well for switching places with two roles for each situation.

Role 1: Someone who is injured or sick and can't walk or get food for themselves. How do you feel as that person and what do you need from others? **Role 2:** As a person who could help, what could you offer to ease your friend's suffering?

Role 1: Someone who is very sad because they have lost a beloved pet—can you talk about how you would feel? **Role 2:** Someone who tries to offer comfort and cheer the other up. What ideas can you come up with that might help your friend?

Role 1: Shy basketball player who often stays in the background. He or she misses a key shot that loses a big game. Talk about how you feel as that person. **Role 2:** Star basketball player at school who has had a great game. How can you be a true team player and what can you say and do to help make your teammate feel better?

Role 1: Your next-door neighbor, who's been like a grandmother to you, finds that her flower garden has been severely damaged in a storm. Her flowers are like her children and she's heartbroken. **Role 2:** You've never been a big fan of flowers yourself, but it's clear your neighbor is sad. How can you console her, and is there any action you can take to ease her pain?

Variations on Switching Places:

Not every kid feels comfortable acting, so if role-playing isn't their thing, have your kids write a story about being compassionate one week, and the next, have them draw a picture showing an act of kindness. They can even write a song or a poem or make a compassion collage with words and pictures from magazines that highlight those in need and show ways to help. For older kids, they might prefer to listen to a song like Jewel's "Hands," which has beautiful lyrics about the importance of kindness and the power in each of us to make a difference, even though we think we are insignificant. Or do a family book club and read a book each week. Books like *Hey, Little Ant* by Phillip and Hannah Hoose is great for younger children, or *My Name Is Not Monkey Girl* by Miriam L. Jacobs, or the Dr. Seuss classic *Horton Hears a Who* are wonderful for a second or third grader.

For an older child, read (or watch) the classic Charles Dickens story *A Christmas Carol* for its lessons in the importance of living life with compassion. For a child who could handle more difficult subject matter, *Anne Frank: The Diary of a Young Girl* is both a poignant example of the power of kindness, and the destructive and horrific effects of what can happen when there are those who do not feel any compassion.

One-Time Exercise: At Your Service

Compassion is not about feeling sorry for others. Rather, like respect, compassion is about feeling connected to other people. So at the end of Compassion Month, I recommend an activity that you can do as a family that shows compassion and involves an act of service to others. You might consider visiting a local home for the elderly or bringing meals to an ailing neighbor. It doesn't have to be huge to make a difference in the life of another person. It just has to be rooted in genuine compassion.

There are many ways to practice acts of kindness with your entire family. Here are some suggestions.

- Help an elderly or sick neighbor by raking leaves, sweeping his or her porch, or even taking out his or her garbage.
- Volunteer at your local animal shelter by cuddling and playing with the animals that are waiting to be adopted.
- Put together and send a care package to a man or woman serving in the military.
- Become a foster family for a service dog organization, helping a puppy socialize so that he can help a person who is debilitated in some way.
- Volunteer at a homeless shelter helping to serve food.
- Help build a house for Habitat for Humanity (*www.habitat.org*).
- Knit a blanket, or make a quilt with your family and donate it to the children's ward at your local hospital.
- Read books to vision-impaired people in your community.

- If you have a place of worship, check with them to see what service projects they need help with and then volunteer as a family.

This exercise is purposefully placed at the end of Compassion Month so that children can experience being of service to others, but are always aware that it doesn't stop there. Ideally, this will encourage them to continue to find ways to do good in their communities—and maybe even consider a career in the service of others. As a family, continue to practice acts of kindness long after this month is over so that being of service to others is just a part of your lives.

Variation on At Your Service

Some people feel shy or uncomfortable volunteering, so if you prefer, have a family fundraiser like a garage sale and donate the money you raise to a charity you and your family believe in. Or, just clean out your garage and donate what you can to charity. It's a great opportunity for your kids to see that the toys, books, and clothes that they no longer use can help someone in need. Or set up a lemonade stand with your younger children and donate the money you raise to a charity benefiting kids their age. That way, they are empowered as kids helping other kids. Another way to raise money as a family is to sacrifice a treat, like ordering pizza or going out to a play or concert, and instead give the money you would have spent to charity.

Staying Power

While we waited in line at a popular breakfast restaurant recently, my daughter noticed a canister near the cash register that was displayed to raise money for a local animal shelter. For some reason she had brought along all her money that day, and although it was only loose change, it was everything she had. Completely on her own, she put it all in the canister declaring that she did it because she "cares for the animals."

After Compassion Month, I heard about a family who had lost their home because of a flood. I knew it was a call to action, so the kids and I went shopping. We sent teddy bears, along with cuddly blankets and other toys and supplies for the children in the family. It did my heart good to see my kids carefully choosing just the right toys and teddy bears for children they didn't even know and would probably never meet. But I knew that didn't matter.

But how do you hold on to the lessons of this month when your life is so busy already? What if you simply don't have the time to volunteer very often, or the financial resources to make donations to those in need? Here's the answer. Compassion doesn't have to be reserved only for other people. Of course, I strongly encourage you to try to reach out and be compassionate and kind beyond your own family. But like respect, compassion starts at home. Maybe your son isn't going to be raking the neighbors lawn very often after this month is over, but he can still notice when his younger sister needs cheering up or when Dad has had a bad day at work and could use a kind word. And you can give him a big hug and make him his favorite dinner on a day he came in last in a swim meet. There are countless ways to show compassion in your own family every day and you're probably already doing them without even realizing it. If you're not, start making these small acts a part of your life. As long as you remember to do this, you will never leave this value behind.

Month Six

FORGIVENESS

Letting go of hurts and grudges

As a parent, this is a value you really need! Think about it. There are times when your kids drive you crazy and sometimes you snap at them for no apparent reason. It happens to all of us. Or, one of your kids spills a can of paint on the living room carpet and feels so terrible about it they can't even speak. Actually, I'm having a flashback—I did that when I was six. But I digress. Plain and simple—you are going to need this value.

Everybody makes mistakes, and if we get caught up in being upset with our partners or our kids, or ourselves for that matter, we're gonna be stuck. And nobody wants to be stuck, even if they were right and the other person was 100 percent wrong. So there. The bottom line is, teaching your children how to move on and forgive, as well as how to accept forgiveness, is crucial. This month will give you specific tools to do just that.

So many people carry around a lifelong burden of grudges and bitterness that inevitably holds them back in so many ways. You undoubtedly want your children to be unencumbered by such a burden, and to enjoy the sense of freedom that comes from truly being able to forgive. However, it's important that children learn that forgiving someone is not the same thing as saying that the hurtful thing done to them is acceptable, or even allowable. This is an important message for children.

Many of us know well-meaning people who allow themselves to be treated as doormats because they see themselves as being very forgiving people. They let others walk all over them again and again in the name of forgiveness. Forgiveness should never be self-destructive. It's important for children to find a way to sincerely forgive people who let them down without allowing for a pattern of hurt and disappointment to take over. Sometimes that means forgiving someone for truly hurting them and then no longer letting that person be a part of their lives. In that way, though it may not be easy, they can stop the pattern of hurt and let go of the burden of anger and resentment and try to move on with their lives in a healthy way.

It is equally important to teach your children to learn how to be forgiven. Because, let's face it, sometimes they are the ones who have messed up and are in need of forgiveness. When that happens, it's healthy to seek forgiveness and to accept it when it comes rather than continuing to berate themselves. Sometimes that can be very hard for kids to do. That's one of the reasons Self-Respect Month comes before Forgiveness Month. That way if, your kids are overwhelmed by guilt or feelings of recrimination, and get too hard on themselves, you can refer back to what they learned about self-respect and get them back on track. Self-respect doesn't come from seeing ourselves as perfect. Instead, it requires us to accept and love ourselves, and to forgive ourselves when we inevitably make mistakes. It's not productive to hold ourselves up to impossible standards. If the standards are impossible, no one could live up to them, so we have to accept the fact that we will let others down sometimes and we have to learn to forgive ourselves.

For one thing, if we can see ourselves as human beings who make mistakes and deserve forgiveness, then we can see others like that as well. And if we see mistakes as opportunities to learn, and to make better choices in the future, then we have made some progress.

There is great power in forgiveness. Learning how to forgive others, and ourselves, is extremely important. As parents, you hate to think that anyone will hurt your children's feelings, but of course it happens. And inevitably, sometimes it is your own children who do the hurting. I admit, I used to be one of those moms who would urge my kids to apologize when they had done something wrong. As I look back on all those times my husband and I insisted that our children say they were sorry, I realize that we were once again guilty of training our kids to "say" the right thing rather than "do" the right thing, just like we had done with equating saying "Thank you" with being grateful.

Now, we approach this much differently. When Connor says something hurtful to Grace, for instance, instead of urging him to apologize right away, we ask that he take some time to consider her feelings and think about how powerful his words are to her. Generally speaking, when we give him the time and space and guidance to think about the impact of what he has said or done, he comes up with a beautiful and genuine apology on his own. And what if he doesn't, you say? Well, is no apology much worse than an insincere one? I don't think so. We've all been on the receiving end of an insincere apology and it only makes the wound deeper. What's the point in that? Later, in our weekly exercise, you'll learn to teach your kids how to apologize in a way that is sincere and has meaning.

It's also important to teach children the power to forgive others in their own lives. But it's not easy to learn how to forgive. Didn't Alexander Pope write the now famous words, "To err is human. To forgive, divine?" How do we get ourselves, let alone our kids, to aspire to something that lofty? The answer is, we don't. At least not at first.

The Freedom of Forgiveness

Start by talking to your kids about what it feels like to carry a grudge and withhold forgiveness. It's a burden. Do they want to carry around that burden for a long time or do they want to just let it go? At this point, they'll inevitably bring up the idea that if they forgive the person, then it feels as if somehow they are just letting that person off the hook and saying that what the person did was okay. That's a common misperception about forgiveness. Look at it this way—often people don't even care if they are forgiven. Some people can be careless and hurtful with another person's feelings and just go on about their day without looking back. So being forgiven or not being forgiven doesn't really matter to someone like that. But if your children are the ones who have been hurt, then forgiving or not forgiving matters to them because they are the ones who will be carrying around that anger, bitterness, and resentment. All that stuff is heavy, and they'll be the ones carrying it, not the person who hurt them. Forgiving someone is often about relieving your own burden, rather than that of someone else.

When I talk to my kids about this, they inevitably bring up another point. They're upset and mad that the other person doesn't care about hurting them! Well, of course, if that's the case, it's out of their control. The upside to this is that if you don't have control over everything, you also don't have responsibility for everything. So if someone feels no remorse, you can't make him or her be sorry, but that's okay. It's not your responsibility to do that. You can just let it go. There is tremendous power in that.

The great thing about forgiveness is the emotional freedom that comes with it. That freedom is much better than anything materialistic you could ever give to your kids. The ability to forgive others as well as themselves and being able to accept forgiveness can remove many obstacles in their lives. So, now that you have started to talk to your kids about forgiveness, you are ready to move on to this month's exercises, which will help them go deeper into the experience of forgiving and being forgiven.

What You Need for This Month's Exercises:

- This month, you'll only need supplies for the one-time exercise. You'll need a beach ball or a large pillow. Anything soft and yet kind of bulky will work. Feel free to improvise!

Daily Exercise: Letting Go

Each day of Forgiveness Month, the Letting Go Exercise will give you and your children the opportunity to put the idea of forgiveness into practice. Every night before they go to bed, ask your kids to forgive someone; parents should participate too. The important thing is to have each member of the family let go of a hurtful thing each day. For your kids, typically, it will be a small offense that may have happened that day or even a while ago; maybe something they've been hanging on to. It could be a classmate who shoved them aside during recess, a sibling who pinched them or called them a name, a grownup who seemed too busy to really listen to them, or even, and often most importantly, themselves.

Have them say aloud what they are going to forgive and why. Then ask them to say, "I let it go." Ask them to imagine that when they don't forgive someone, even for a something minor, it's like carrying around a pebble for each small offense. Pretty soon all those little pebbles get heavy. Each night, ask your kids to imagine tossing one of those pebbles into a big ocean as they say, "I let it go." By applying an image of what it can be like to let go of even small grudges and to imagine those pebbles getting swept away by the ocean, forgiveness feels more *real* to them.

One mom, Beth, who experienced Forgiveness Month with her two sons, ages eight and eleven, found that they would sometimes talk about forgiving something while they were in the car. She said her boys would just roll down the windows and imagine throwing their "pebbles" out. Or sometimes one of her sons would imagine using a rocket launcher to send any resentment he had way off into the distance where he could "see" it blow up.

If your kids are struggling with something ongoing, or a hurt that seems too significant to let go of in this way, of course, listen to them and let them know that if they choose, they may want to work on that during the one-time exercise at the end of the month. If they prefer to talk about it right then, listen and help them sort through whatever they are dealing with.

Variations on Letting Go

If your children are hesitant to say out loud who or what they want to forgive, you can let them write down the things they let go each night. They might write down, "I forgive my dad for not playing catch today like he said he would." Then, have them put the slip of paper in an empty shoebox each night. At the end of the month, they can "let go" of everything by discarding the box and its contents. For an older child, they may prefer to keep a list of things they forgive each night. The idea of the exercise is to get kids to understand the importance of letting things go before the issues build up and get overwhelming. It is about giving kids practice at being forgiving.

Weekly Exercise: Will You Forgive Me?

Since the daily exercise focuses on forgiving, the weekly exercise deals with the flip side—apologizing sincerely and then being able to accept forgiveness. Once a week during this month, give everyone the opportunity to be forgiven by someone else in the family. Inevitably, something has happened that week that may need forgiving, and it may be something you didn't even know about.

During this exercise, each person must say what they are sorry for, using a specific apology structure. An apology shouldn't stop at the words "I'm sorry." It has to go beyond that. When doing this exercise, and in everyday life, ask your children (and follow the same guidelines for yourself) to say *what* each of you is sorry for. If your son was blasting music while his sister was trying to do her homework, he could say, "I apologize for playing my CD so loudly."

Then, take it one step further, and here's where it becomes a very individualized and personal thing. The apology must extend one sentence beyond the, "I'm sorry for . . . " part and that sentence has to relate to what happened. That's all the guidance you should give. Including one more sentence in an apology can serve two purposes. First of all, it often gives the person who has been wronged some context for what happened. Secondly, you'll often see your children reach out to try and make amends with that additional sentence. So your son might say, "I'm sorry for playing my CD so loudly. Next time, I'll be quieter."

In my house, we have found that having the time and space to be ready to make an apology and then having the structure in which to frame that apology has made all the difference in our family. There has been a surprising benefit for us in having this structure for apologies. When we started this, I thought it would encourage all of us to go beyond simply saying "I'm sorry" and therefore give the apology more depth and context. What I didn't realize at the time, and what my son has since pointed out to me is that it also provides *limits* to an apology. In other words, an apology doesn't have to be ten minutes long to express how very, very, very sorry you are for something. The apology can be just a few sincere and heartfelt sentences. What a relief, especially for a kid!

As you do this exercise, take the opportunity to talk about doing your best not to repeat the offense. That shows you care about each other's feelings and you try to learn from your mistakes.

Beth and her sons, mentioned earlier in this chapter, found this exercise to be very helpful. She said it made her boys, especially her older son, much more aware that his actions might be hurtful to others. Once he was aware of that, he could apologize sincerely.

Variations on Will You Forgive Me?

The point of this exercise is that everyone in the family has an opportunity to apologize and be forgiven for something. But your child may not want to admit that he or she has done something wrong in front of the whole family. In that case, the child could simply ask to talk to his or her sibling, or you or your partner more privately and the forgiveness could be given in a way that everyone doesn't hear. The exercises should never be a source of embarrassment for a child (or an adult, for that matter).

Another way to do this exercise would be to write a short note with an apology (using the guidelines in this exercise) and give it to the person who has been hurt or let down. Then that person should write a note in return offering forgiveness when they are ready. Ideally, the exercise is done in a way that works best for the personalities of the people in the family. If needed, mix and match these suggestions so that everyone finds a format that is comfortable for them. In that case, though, try to keep the apology and the forgiveness in the same format.

One-Time Exercise: "The Rock"

As mentioned earlier in this chapter, without being able to forgive others who have hurt us, or even ourselves for mistakes we have made, we are essentially carrying a heavy burden throughout our lives. Sometimes, kids may struggle with the idea of forgiveness because they are dealing with an ongoing or a more difficult issue. Please keep in mind that you should never push your children to forgive—especially if the issue is too complicated or upsetting for them to deal with. These may be the times you seek the help of an expert, such as a counselor, therapist, or clergy person, to assist you and your child. This exercise is simply to help children process the idea that they can be capable of forgiveness even if the issue feels bigger to them than a minor day-to-day offense.

And it's not always easy to forgive those types of things. In this exercise, ask everyone in your family to think of one of those tougher issues. Then, one by one, have each person take a turn at holding a large beach ball or cushion that

Month Six

serves as the "rock" or burden that they carry when they won't forgive. The "rock" may not be heavy, but it still acts as an encumbrance as they try to hold on to it for more than a few minutes. Encourage them to walk around the room and try to do the things they normally would be doing, such as watching TV, reading a book, or even eating lunch. When the "rock" inevitably gets in their way and becomes a burden, remind them that putting it down is like letting go of any bitterness or resentment they might be feeling. Ask them if they are ready to forgive the big offense, and if so, tell them to let go of the "rock" and move on with their day. But encourage them to hold onto it until they are really ready to forgive or at least have a conversation about what has hurt them.

If they need to talk about it, put the "rock" down for a while. If, after you've talked about it, they think they can forgive, give them back the "rock." They then say what they are forgiving and put down their "burden." In my house, we find this exercise helps our kids to understand how good it feels to let go of something hurtful and to move on with their lives. In many ways, forgiveness is freedom. And that's a powerful thing for a child to realize.

As I mentioned, I do realize that some children may have significant issues to deal with and won't be able to find resolution or a path to forgiveness through this exercise. My intention is not to push anyone into forgiving if they aren't ready. Again, no one should be pressured to forgive. This exercise is meant to show children that when we don't forgive, we are the ones who carry around a burden. Even if they take away that message without feeling that they have forgiven someone, it will still have value to them as they go through life. There may be a time when they are older that the message will become more real and relevant to them.

Variations on "The Rock"

If your children are not keen on this exercise or are not physically able to do it, they can express the idea of being burdened with a grudge and then forgiving someone and letting go of that burden in other ways. They can draw a picture of themselves when they are carrying a big grudge. What does the "grudge" look like? What kind of picture can they draw when they put the grudge down and they are no longer burdened?

Some kids prefer to write down their feelings. If that's your child, have them write a little story about the burden of a grudge and what happens when it is released. The point of the exercise is to show the child, in a concrete way, the difference between holding back on forgiveness and truly forgiving someone.

Staying Power

My daughter has really embraced the spirit of forgiveness in our home. Once after Forgiveness Month, when I was tired and I snapped at her, she stopped and looked at me for a moment. I took a breath, apologized for being short with her, and explained that she deserved my full attention. "That's okay, Mom," she said. "I forgive you. You wanna play paper dolls with me?" She was over it. No grudge there.

One of the most important lessons I have personally taken away from Forgiveness Month is that most of the time, people do the best they can. It's as simple as that. We can feel upset when a friend forgets a lunch date or we can forgive her and understand that she is a frazzled, overworked mom who has too many things on her mind. Am I going to carry a grudge? No way. So she let me down. She did the best she could. Next time, I'll take lunch over to her house or offer to watch her kids so she can go have a quiet, peaceful lunch by herself. That's infinitely better than walking around feeling wronged.

After this month is over, if you hear your children talking about something upsetting that happened, remind them about "letting go" and see if they are ready to do so. And continue using the unpressured and structured apology with your kids. This will encourage them to say they are sorry *when* they are sorry. Their apology may not come right away, but when they do say it, it will be real. And whether the apology is accepted or not, they will know they've done their part and they can move on without guilt or recriminations.

As I mentioned at the beginning of this chapter, forgiveness can be an especially important value for moms and dads. Sometimes it seems like we are under constant pressure to do everything right, all the time, or else we're perceived as bad parents. Sometimes that pressure is coming directly *from* us— *to* us. That's the worst kind. It's hard to live up to our own expectations of what it means to be a good parent. No, not a good parent. A great one. But give yourself a break. There may be chocolate syrup all over your laptop, and the path from your back door to the kitchen may be an obstacle course of about fifty-three wooden blocks strewn randomly. That's okay. Unless the queen of England is on her way over, don't worry about it. That's not what being a great mom or dad is about.

Loving your kids and showing that you love them, being there when they fall down, and giving them what is most important to you—your values—is what really matters. So don't be too hard on yourself for all the day-to-day stuff that seems to fall through the cracks. Let it go. Your kids will see that you can forgive yourself and they will know it's okay if they forgive themselves too. Because everyone makes mistakes. It's what happens when we forgive and accept forgiveness that really matters.

Month Seven

A SENSE OF JOY

Celebrating life!

If you're like me, there are probably many things you wish for your children, but a few are universal—that they will be safe and healthy and that these beautiful children whom you love indescribably will have happy lives. Their happiness means everything and their joy becomes an extension of your own. It elevates you and fills your life.

I remember when my son was just a few months old, and a friend asked me what it felt like to be a mom.

"I used to breathe air and now I breathe joy," was my response. It may sound hokey, but that's how it felt to me. Everything had changed.

We parents can get a promotion at work, be elected PTA president in a landslide, and lose ten pounds, and that feels pretty darn great. But when your daughter tells you that playing hopscotch with you made that day the best day she's ever had, or your little boy laughs uncontrollably over your attempt to play a video game with him, you're over the moon. Because you're a parent, and there's something magical about seeing your child truly happy that trumps all that other stuff. Yeah, even the ten pounds. So take a month to focus on this sublime value with your children, and don't stop there. Hold on to the lessons and memories of this month always. Value happiness and your children will learn to value it too.

The Joy of Pennies

When my son was two and a half years old, he taught me a lesson about joy I will never forget. It was an absolutely beautiful autumn morning and the two of us set off to pick out a pumpkin at a local garden center. There were so many things there to grab the attention of a curious toddler—scarecrows, bales of hay, corn stalks, and of course, rows and rows of pumpkins. But the thing that caught Connor's eye was a large water fountain in the center of it all. He was watching as another little boy and his dad tossed a few coins into the water. He asked me why they were throwing their money away.

"They're making wishes," I explained. "Each time they throw in a coin, they make a wish."

My son was fascinated. "Do you have any coins, Mommy?" he asked, looking hopeful.

I looked in my coin purse and I had several pennies, so I grabbed a handful of them and handed one to Connor. I explained to him that each penny could grant him a wish. He couldn't wait to get started. He was moving back and forth from one foot to the other like toddlers do when they're about to burst with excitement. So I quickly showed him how to stand with his back to the fountain so he could make his wish and then throw the penny over his shoulder into the water. He looked down at the penny in his hand, made his wish, and then carefully tossed the coin over his shoulder, delighted when he heard a small splash as it hit the water. He was jumping and squealing with pure joy. Then I handed him another penny and the whole scene played out again. One by one, as he took each coin, it was just as magical for him as it was with the first one. I figured he was excited about all those wishes coming true so I asked him what he had wished for. I didn't expect the answer he gave.

"More pennies!" He said.

Right away, tears sprang to my eyes. It hadn't been about the wishes for him. Not at all. It was all about the experience. There was joy, right there in front of both of us. But he was the only one who knew it. He was the only one who was truly living the joy in that moment. He was inside the joy, surrounded by it, jumping up and down with it, for goodness sake. And there I was, observing it from the outside. I cry now when I think of that moment. Not because I'm sad, but because I'm so grateful for the lesson my son taught me that day. So often joy is right there, but we miss it.

Sometimes even a lesson that profound gets lost in the rush of everyday life. To many people, a sense of joy may not seem like a value. However, it may be one of the most important.

For example, when Connor was ten years old, he started asking us about the meaning of life. My husband and I told him that we believe it is about using the gifts we have been given in our lives in the most joyful way possible. And that's important, because we don't always recognize the gifts we've been given as gifts per se. Sometimes they feel like something we'd rather not have at all. So that's where the joy comes in, or at least a sense of humor. And what's the point of being grateful, compassionate, or respectful if there is no joy in it? If we do these things only out of a sense of obligation, without joy, it diminishes them. Joy is important.

Some children may be puzzled when you tell them that this month's activities focus on the importance of happiness in life. After all, aren't you either happy or not happy? Well, not exactly. As you become consumed with responsibilities and day-to-day life, happiness can take a back seat. And very little slips past your kids. They see everything and they take it all in. If you are encouraging them to be happy and yet you're only going through the motions in life, then that will be a much bigger influence on them than anything you say.

And that brings to mind yet another surface type of message that my husband and I were giving our kids back before we started doing these monthly values. How often have you told your kids to, "Smile!" just because you wanted them to put on a happy face in a roomful of your friends or coworkers? I've said it too many times in the past, but I don't say it anymore. This goes along with the desire to truly go beyond the surface when teaching our children about values. And when it comes to joy, we would much rather that our children *be* happy than merely put on a happy face.

Of course, most parents wish that their children will be happy people. But parents can't *make* children happy. Yes, you can do day-to-day considerate things like making their favorite dinner or bringing home a DVD for the family to watch together. But when it comes to a deep and abiding happiness, each of us must find that within ourselves.

When you first talk to your kids about happiness, consider explaining this concept of two kinds of happiness. First, there is the joy they may feel when they have a wonderful time picking apples with the whole family on a gorgeous fall day, or roller skating with friends even though they fall down a lot, or playing a board game with their grandma.

But what about that deeper kind of happiness? You would think that would be harder to explain to a child, but in my experience, like with the pennies in the fountain, they often have a much better understanding of this kind of happiness than we do as grownups. Think of it this way: when was the last time you, as an adult, happily skipped down the street? Parents (and by "parents" I mean "me") sometimes fill up their children's lives with so much stuff, and so much entertainment, that the kids don't have the opportunity to experience true, simple happiness as much as they should. If you're like me, you *always* bring copious amounts of puzzle books, toys, or games to keep your kids busy at restaurants or doctor's offices. I am guilty of over-entertaining my kids. In fact, it pains me deeply to admit that once on vacation, as we waited several minutes for an elevator that turned out to be broken, my son turned to me and asked, "Do you have an activity for this, Mom?" Yikes. As parents, we sometimes get so caught up in trying to make our children happy that we attempt to fill every potential moment of boredom with something entertaining. Now I'm not suggesting that you go to the dentist's office unprepared. Forty-five minutes in a waiting room with a six-year-old can age you prematurely! But in my case, I took it way too far—and I'm guessing other parents have too. And in circumventing any possibility for my kids to be bored, I took away the chance for them to find something in their imagination or environment that would interest them. I didn't let them make their own happiness and I misled them into expecting that fun and fascinating activities would always be provided for them in life. Not only that, while they were busy with their puzzle books, they could have been interacting with *us*.

Because it helps to deepen the understanding of why we do these exercises, when we began the discussion about Sense of Joy Month, we explained to our kids that living a joyful life is not merely about being a happy person. It's also important to spread joy to those around you. The goal of this month is to inspire this kind of joyful living in our children. In order to achieve this, start with a simple and fun daily exercise that encourages children to make joy a priority in their lives.

Supplies for This Month's Exercises:

- Index cards in various colors and a smile!

Daily Exercise: Don't Hurry, Be Happy

At the beginning of the month, everyone in the family gets colorful index cards and writes down several little things that make them happy. In total, there should be one card for each day of the month—so roughly thirty. Write down quick things like dancing to lively music, telling a joke, singing a silly song . . . whatever each person finds joyful. It can also be something you don't necessarily think of as "fun," but is something that can bring joy, like taking a moment as a family to admire a beautiful flower in your garden, getting out an art book and looking at a photograph of a Renoir painting, or passing around a lovely little shell you brought back from vacation. If it brings you joy, and you can share that joy with your family for a few moments every day this month, it will be ideal for this exercise. Put all of the cards in a large vase or bowl and keep it somewhere in your kitchen or living room where it's easy to access each day.

Each morning at breakfast (or whatever time works best for your family's schedule), ask one person to pull one of these joyful suggestions out of the bowl. Then, the whole family does whatever the card says. If you've chosen something that takes a little longer to do—or requires some planning, like finding a joke to tell—simply do it later in the day. The best part about this, aside from the silliness that sometimes happens, is that, of course, someone ends up doing an activity that someone else wrote down, and it might not be his or her idea of fun or joy at all. Yet inevitably, it turns out to be special for the entire family because everyone gets a sense of what gives other family members true joy.

Here are some other ideas for activities that you can do with your family:

- Find a short, family-friendly, silly video on the Internet and watch it with your whole family before the kids head off to school.
- Try talking in pig Latin during breakfast.
- If you or your child is musically inclined, take five minutes to play a song on the piano or guitar or even the kitchen countertop! Everyone should join in making music in his or her own way—make it a family jam session.
- Take out a book of riddles or print some from the Internet and have each person read one to the family.
- Put on a song from the 1960s and do the twist.
- Have everyone in the family try to say a tongue twister together.
- Take out your camera and have everyone take a picture of something in the house that he or she thinks is beautiful, or go outside if you have outdoor space and photograph the beauty that you each see.
- Listen to Beethoven's inspiring "Ode to Joy" while you're eating breakfast. Or create a playlist on your MP3 player with happy classic tunes like Louis Armstrong performing "What a Wonderful World," "Don't Worry, Be Happy" by Bobby McFerrin, "Walking on Sunshine" by Katrina and the Waves, or Neil Diamond's "I'm A Believer."
- Have everyone try drawing a self-portrait using his or her nondominant hand.
- Buy the silliest straws you can find at the dollar store and hand then out to everyone to use at breakfast.
- Play hopscotch in the house.

- Make the goofiest-shaped pancakes you can think of and decorate them with bits of fruit like blueberries and bananas, or be extra silly and use peas!
- Have everyone speak with a foreign accent during breakfast.
- Using one of those soft balls, play a game of dodge ball indoors—put away the breakables and try to stay away from the lamps!
- Take a few minutes to look at beautiful black-and-white nature photographs.
- Read a funny short story. Have everyone read a page and then pass the story to the next person.
- Play jump rope with the whole family.
- Count your blessings with your kids (one of my son's suggestions).
- If you have someone in your family who creates beautiful works of art—like handmade quilts—spend a few moments really looking at them and noticing their beauty.
- Print out a funny scene from a movie like the famous one by Abbott and Costello, "Who's on First," and perform it with your kids.
- Have a family hug.
- Start a silly story where one member of the family contributes a few lines and stops in the middle of a sentence, then the next person continues the story, giving it their own silly twist and so on. . . .
- Play a quick game of Twister.
- Have everyone eat something silly like my daughter's invention—raw carrots with whipped cream on top!
- Play one of those handclapping games like "Double, Double" or "Miss Mary Mack."
- Play musical chairs at breakfast.

- Do silly walks as you head off to take the kids to catch the morning school bus. See who can be silliest.
- Have family karaoke night. Just put on a song that each member of the family knows and have them sing it on "stage" using spoons for microphones.
- Play "Telephone," where one person whispers a really short story to another person and that continues until everyone has heard the story. Then reveal what the original story was and see how far off it became.
- Do the Tango!

One of the best things about this exercise for my family has been that we each bring something of ourselves to it. For instance, I don't think my kids knew how important things like classical music and fine art were to me before we started doing this exercise. But when I got my turn to share this with them, they not only got a chance to appreciate something I personally find beautiful, they got a chance to know me better. Who knows what your children will be surprised to learn about you?

Parents Karen and Jeff participated in Sense of Joy Month with their two daughters, ages five and seven. On the first day, the girls picked an index card that read, "Be a tickle monster." They had such a great time with that one that the girls found a way to keep picking that card day after day. Karen and her husband just went along with it because the family was truly experiencing the point of the exercise: to bring a little fun and joy into every day. Karen told me that she doubts her girls will ever forget the experience.

You don't have to have everyone in the family give their ideas if you prefer to come up with them yourself and surprise your kids each day with what you'll be doing. Or you could stick with one theme like "dance of the day" or joke of the day." As long as your kids get the message that it's good to break up the daily routine with something fun or joyful, that's the important thing. The key is to enjoy yourselves and have fun every day this month and hopefully, you'll make it a habit!

Weekly Exercise: Make Someone Happy

Once a week during this month each member of the family should do something that they know brings happiness to someone else in the family. Maybe your son might agree to play his sister's favorite board game even though it's not his favorite. Or perhaps your daughter might join you for an evening walk to the park when she'd rather stay home and watch a movie, because she knows how much you enjoy her company. Parents take part too. You can finger paint with your daughter because she has so much fun being artistic, or go swimming with your son because he loves being in the water. Explain to your kids that this exercise shows them some ways that they can bring happiness into the lives of others.

Point out that it isn't necessarily possible to make someone else feel that deeper kind of happiness, but that you can do things to bring joy to people every day. Some other ideas for things your family can do for each other include:

- Grownups: Play with your children! Go outside and go for a bike ride or roast marshmallows on a bonfire and tell stories. Or make crafts with them or show them how to take pictures with a point-and-shoot camera.
- Cuddle up and watch a movie with your kids
- If Dad is into sports, one of the non–sports-loving kids in the family could watch a baseball game with him and even put out snacks just to make Dad happy
- An older sibling could make breakfast in bed for a younger sibling and prepare his or her favorite food.
- Dad and the kids can bake Mom's favorite dessert.
- Mom can let the kids style her hair and pick out Dad's outfit for the day.
- The kids can draw a bath for Mom and put aside her favorite magazine for her to read while relaxing in the bath.

The point of this exercise is to show children how important it is for them to extend themselves in order to bring joy to other people in their lives. The side benefit is that you may notice your children feeling happy doing things for other people.

Variations on Make Someone Happy:

Ideally, doing something that brings joy to another family member is the main idea behind this exercise. But your kids could also do something to bring happiness to someone outside the immediate family, such as a teacher, friend, or grandparent. So your daughter could invite a friend to play a new game she hasn't played herself yet or your son could make a silly card to give to the teacher on a Monday morning. Or, both kids could hang out at Grandma's because they love her and they know that being with them brings her joy.

One-Time Exercise: Joy in Doing

Exuberance is not a passive emotion. There is something about doing a joyful thing that takes it to the next level and that's what Sense of Joy Month is all about. After all, isn't it much more enjoyable and interesting to participate in something rather than watch something fun happening? So once during this month, make a conscious effort to do something you know the whole family will enjoy. Sometimes, you might need to plan something, while other times, spontaneity is key! Most importantly, this is an activity for the whole family to experience together.

When we participated in Sense of Joy at my house it was July, and we were sitting at home listening to the sounds of fireworks all around our neighborhood. We couldn't quite see anything from our house because of trees. It was past bedtime and my son and daughter were already in their pajamas, but suddenly I said, "Get in the car. We're going to see the fireworks!" The kids were surprised, but they happily jumped in the car and we drove a few blocks to the park. Barely able to see the fireworks through the trees, I yelled out, "To the top of the slide!" Both kids ran up the slide as fast as they could. What a view! We kept turning in circles to see all the different fireworks from the surrounding communities. When they were over, we all slid down the slide. None of us will ever forget it. That's joy, pure and simple.

Here are some ideas for other things you can do with your family for this exercise:

- Attend an outdoor concert. Bring a big blanket and a festive picnic dinner with unexpected treats and new things for your kids to taste.
- Go on a family camping trip and spend time fishing and hiking together.
- Spend a night at the museum with your family—some museums have overnight programs available now, especially for members.
- Have a party! Invite people to bring their favorite appetizers and then get together with your family to prepare the main course together. Come up with a theme, decorate the house, and prepare a fun dessert together.
- Go horseback riding with the family.

Variations on Joy in Doing:

If you prefer to stay home, try putting on a play with your kids or having a pillow fight. Or go outside and run through the sprinklers with your kids. When is the last time you did that? Remember that this exercise doesn't need to cost a penny or require a road trip to be memorable and fun for your family. When you are doing the exercises this month with your kids, don't neglect yourself. Be sure to do the exercises too. Dance and sing. Be silly and spontaneous.

Staying Power

My daughter is one of those people who loves to make others happy. She brings me treats and loves to make things special in order to bring a smile to my face.

The wonderful thing about this is that when we make other people happy, we can't help but feel good ourselves. That's one of the lessons of Sense of Joy Month that I encourage you to hold onto. Of course, there has to be balance to it. Too often as parents, we get so caught up in trying to make our children happy that we forget about our own joy. Make happiness a priority for the whole family, yourself included.

By making joy an important part of your own daily life, it shows your kids what an important value this really is. Continue to take the time to do many joyful things with your children after this month is over. And remember that being a parent can and should be a joyful experience. It's not all changing diapers, making school lunches, and carpooling. But wait just a minute. Take a look at those things. If you consider them to be mundane chores, think again. They are all opportunities for joy. Tickle your baby when you change his diaper. Put silly notes in your child's lunchbox. Insist on singing '80s songs to the kids in your car. Sure, your kids may be embarrassed. But they just might start giggling along with their friends in the car. And you'll be singing, so hey—you're having fun. Just don't try any dance moves until you get out of the car!

Month Eight

COMMITMENT

Doing what you said you'd do, when you said you'd do it

At least 200 percent of being a parent has to do with commitment. Maybe more. When your five-year-old son wakes up at 3:24 A.M. after having a nightmare, you are there, in his room, holding him until he falls asleep. And the next morning at 7:00, bleary eyed, you're making breakfast for your kids. You're a parent and you have commitments every day, and you do your best to keep them. That's what this month is all about. You've seen firsthand what the power of commitment has meant in your life as a parent. Now this month you will be able to share that with your kids. It's their turn to keep commitments. And, as in past months, you may be surprised at what they can do.

When I was a child, my mother would often say, "Never break a promise." In our house, and in our family, a promise was almost a sacred thing. Nowadays, it can be hard to find people who believe that promises and commitments are important. But my family still strives to take promises seriously, whether they are made to a friend, a coworker, or to each other. And boy, do our kids know it. Whether we promise to take them out to a movie on a particular day, or to take away their toys if they don't clean up after themselves, we keep our promises.

But what exactly is the difference between a commitment and a promise? First, a commitment can take you much further than a one-time promise. Let's say your nine-year-old daughter promises to go to piano practice early on Saturday morning, and she does it. Great. That's nice. But that doesn't mean she can play the piano. That takes a commitment. That means she gets up Saturday morning after Saturday morning for quite some time—probably years. Then you may have a piano player. Actually, you have more than that. You have a child who understands the power of keeping a commitment—that is, if the commitment was hers in the first place.

And here's the thing. If your nine-year-old daughter hates piano lessons, she may be keeping your commitment by going to lessons every Saturday morning, but she's not keeping her own. And that's an important distinction. Most parents are quite busy keeping their own commitments. This month is about allowing our children to make—and keep—commitments on their own.

Since this yearlong journey is about always striving to go to the deepest level when teaching values to your children, Commitment Month goes well beyond teaching them just to keep promises. The goal is for them to understand what making a commitment really means. To make a commitment is to take on the responsibility of keeping an ongoing promise. Since you have explored the importance of promises in Integrity Month, you can build on that. You'll also find that the exercises this month, as well as the conversations you'll have, address the idea of responsibility—a sense of ownership and accountability. It's important for children to take ownership of their actions. As a parent, it may be difficult to let a child take responsibility for him or herself when you know you could do whatever it is so much better and faster. But it's not about you. Unless you intend to be one of those "helicopter parents," hovering ever so closely around your kids' lives well into their adulthoods, this isn't a good idea.

To make the idea of responsibilities and commitment real to younger children, consider using visual aids. That's what I did with my daughter. I got out a small bucket and some little plastic balls and Grace and I sat down on the floor and talked about the things that she is responsible for, like attending school, doing her homework, caring for her kitten, and putting away her toys. I had her put a ball in the bucket for each responsibility and I explained that being responsible for something means that she alone is in charge of making sure it gets done. I reassured her that I have confidence in her ability to take on responsibilities, but that she has to think about what she can handle and how it is possible to take on too many things. The bucket can fill up pretty fast!

You can try this as well. For example, if your son is on a baseball team and he has practice twice a week, it's his responsibility to be there, so you would put in a ball for each practice. Another ball each for school, violin lessons, and computer club. Eventually, as you cover all of your child's responsibilities, the bucket may overflow. You may share a laugh about this, but there's a serious lesson in there. Talk about how that bucket is like a place where your child could imagine putting all of his commitments—the ongoing promises he agrees to be responsible for. Explain how it's important not to make too many commitments, because if you do, you can't keep them—like the balls in the bucket, they overflow out of control.

So now, if your child wants to join another club or take on an added responsibility, he can check that little bucket to make sure he can handle it. And if he really wants to join the soccer team, that might mean taking out the ball for baseball so that the bucket doesn't overflow. Many parents could learn a thing or two from that bucket!

If you don't have the supplies mentioned above, just ask your child to visualize filling the bucket with responsibilities and talk about it.

Explaining the idea of commitment can be a little different when it comes to older children. You can use a dry erase board and ask your child to write down his commitments as he takes them on, or you can just sit down and talk when he feels that he might be ready to take on a new responsibility.

So, are there ever times when it's okay to break a commitment? Yes, I think so. If your child commits to be on a team, but then gets injured, it is not in the best interest of his health and safety to continue playing that sport, at least until his injury heals. If your daughter commits to being in a dance recital, but after a few rehearsals you get word from another parent or your own child that the director is being verbally abusive to the children, it certainly may be time to take action. If the school won't assign a new director, then that's the time to talk to your child about it and make a decision about whether to take her out of that activity. Generally, if a situation where children have made a commitment becomes in any way detrimental to their physical, emotional, or mental well-being, then it's time to walk away. If they are being disrespected, it's not healthy for them to continue. This goes back to the lessons they learned about respect. No one ever wants their child to feel trapped or stuck in a situation that is not healthy for them.

On the other hand, if the activity requires more time or responsibility than they had originally expected, you may want to encourage them to keep the commitment they made. Don't force them to stay the course, as it's not your commitment—it's theirs. And one of the goals this month is to teach our children that a commitment isn't something made with good intentions at the time and then tucked away in a drawer somewhere. It's real, it's vital, and they should own it.

This month helps to teach children that a commitment begins with a strong belief in whatever they commit themselves to. In other words, when it comes right down to it, a commitment isn't just about the fact that "you said you'd do it" but it is also about the fact that you believed in whatever it was enough to commit in the first place.

So how do you teach a child to keep a commitment? Do you tell them, "Do this or you're in big trouble?" In my experience, that doesn't work. I have found that this is one of those times when a natural consequence can be really helpful. So instead of punishing a child for not keeping a commitment, let the natural consequence simply occur. In other words, just let the child live with his decision to do something or not do something, without intervening. So essentially, we teach by doing nothing, for a change. The exercise for this month illustrates a natural consequence.

Supplies for This Month's Exercises:

- A small plant or a packet of seeds
- A small bag of soil and a plant container with drainage for the daily exercise
- A few sheets of plain or construction paper or even card-stock for the weekly exercise

Daily Exercise: A Living Commitment

This is a very simple exercise that a child of almost any age can do. It involves a plant, sunlight, and water, and that's it!

Each of your children should select his or her small plant (and a watering can) at the store. Explain to your children that each of them is completely responsible for their lovely new plant. Put each plant in the child's bedroom. Make sure your kids understand the watering and care instructions that come with the plant, and then let them take over. It is their job to keep that living commitment to the plants. Don't remind your children to water the plant once during the entire month. In fact, do not interfere in any way.

The wonderful thing about this particular exercise is that, no matter the outcome, it cannot fail to teach the child something. Either they get an understanding of the rewards of honoring their commitment and a boost in pride for being the sole person responsible for keeping this living thing alive, or they understand the natural consequence of not keeping their commitment if the plant dies. Either way, it is a lesson that stays with them.

Lori and Kevin, parents of a four-year-old daughter and an eight-year-old son did Commitment Month with their family. They were doing this exercise with their son and were impressed with how seriously he took his responsibility to his plant. He actually came up with a watering schedule, deciding to water twice a week on Mondays and Fridays. But when he checked the soil on a Sunday night and realized it was still moist, he asked his mom if it was okay to change the watering schedule. She reminded him it was completely his decision, since it was his responsibility. Her son thought about it and decided that he would change his watering days. That decision was his alone—he took total responsibility for it. Pretty cool, I'd say.

For older children, this can be a good time to talk about what commitment means in terms of relationships. For instance, if your daughter makes a commitment to go over to a friend's house and then just decides at the last minute to cancel, there are consequences. Her friend's feelings will most likely be hurt and if this is a pattern, she may lose the friend altogether. That is the natural consequence of not taking care of the friendship. Most kids have probably been on the receiving end of a broken commitment themselves, so they know how it feels.

Variations on a Living Commitment:

Younger children might prefer to start by planting a seed instead of starting with a plant. It makes the exercise a bit more exciting for them because they can see the changes as the seed turns into a seedling and then a "grownup" plant. In that case, you may want to soak the seeds in warm water overnight to give them a good start. Then you can explain to the child how to plant the seed and take care of it. Then leave it up to the child. Or if you start with a small plant, you can encourage your child to choose one that will flower because that can help them to see "progress" as the month goes on.

Weekly Exercise: The Contract

One of the goals of Commitment Month is for children to understand that there are a few different ways that they can establish a commitment. They can make an oral promise to themselves or someone else or they can make it more formal and write it down, which is sometimes more effective. So, during Commitment Month, work with your children to write up a contract in which they commit to do something in particular once each week. Depending on how you do this exercise, parents can also sign a contract to keep a commitment to their children, or they can participate by following through with any agreed upon circumstances.

Sometimes during this year of teaching values, you'll be able to point out to your kids ways to continue living the values you've already focused on, such as self-respect and respect for others. During this month, through The Contract exercise, encourage your children to see that keeping their surroundings clean and orderly can build upon those values. Have a discussion about a commitment they feel they can honor, like cleaning their rooms every Saturday morning. Don't leave it at that, though. Kids are more likely to succeed when you are specific about things. Creating a document such as "The Clean My Room Contract" that both the child and the parents sign really helps. On the contract, number each of the specific responsibilities that your child is committing to such as putting all toys back on their respective shelves, making their bed, and picking up dirty clothes and putting them in the hamper. The words "clean your room" can seem vague and open to interpretation to a kid, but this list of specific responsibilities eliminates confusion. The document we drew up in our family looks like this:

The Clean My Room Contract

My room is the one place in the house that is just for me. So, I can choose to live in it any way I want during the week. But because I share the house with the rest of my family and I don't want anyone to trip and fall on all the stuff I leave on my bedroom floor, I promise to clean my room once a week all by myself with no whining or complaining.

I hereby commit to do the following things every Saturday morning and to do it in one-half hour or less from start to finish. Mom or Dad will start a timer. Other than that, they agree to stay out of it. This is my commitment.

Pick up any stray clothes on my bedroom floor and put them in the laundry basket

Put all books in the bookshelf—neatly

Put all toys and games in the toy closet

Take any glasses or cups and put them in the kitchen sink

Make my bed

Take a paper towel and dust the bookcase, side table, and dresser

Once you have agreed to the exact wording on the document, make sure each child reads through his or her contract before they sign it. After you sign it as well, post the contract on each child's bedroom door.

When Saturday morning (or whatever designated time) comes around, that's when it can get tough, especially for the parents, because you have to stay out of it. You can ask your kids if they would like you to start a timer, if they need one. If they require help getting cleaning supplies, it's perfectly fine for you to put them within your child's reach. But that's as far as you can go. What's the point of a child making a commitment if you don't expect them to honor it? If you are constantly hovering around them, urging them to pick up their socks and helping them make their beds you have shown them that you have an expectation of failure. If you end up approaching the situation that way, it's never going to work. You'll just be teaching them that they don't have to keep their commitments on their own, because Mom or Dad will always be there to make sure they don't fail. The problem with that approach is that you are not in fact helping them in any way. Instead, you are actually setting them up to fail. Even if the commitment is kept, if they didn't do it by themselves, then they've accomplished nothing.

Kids are smart. They'll figure out really fast if you will keep their commitments for them. They often stop trying, because what's the point? So as hard as it is, you have to trust them to keep up their end of the bargain. Believing in them is part of the deal. It is up to them to either keep or break this commitment.

So where are the consequences if they don't honor their commitment to clean their rooms? Well, if their contract says they will put their dirty clothes in the laundry basket and they don't—then don't do their laundry. If they don't keep their commitment, they face the natural consequence of not having any clean clothes to wear, not to mention clean underwear! Allowing them to live as they choose during the week gives them full responsibility for the difficulty of their task on Saturday morning. If they've chosen to be fairly tidy, it's a small amount of work on Saturday, and in no time they can start enjoying their weekend. If they've chosen to be sloppy, they've got their work cut out for them.

Each child is different, and using the natural consequence of having messy clothes may have no effect. They may like going to school in wrinkled, dirty clothes! If natural consequences don't work for your child, you may want to write a specific consequence into the contract. For instance, if they don't keep up their end of the bargain, they get no computer privileges for the week. However, I personally don't recommend rewards for keeping commitments. In my experience, I find that giving rewards for good behavior is not always the best idea. Kids tend to focus a little too much on the reward and not enough on the task. In other words, the reward has much more meaning to them than keeping their commitment, which is what they should be focusing on. Bottom line, whether you use natural or specific consequences isn't as important as doing what is most effective for your own children.

No matter how you structure the contract, it's your job to keep up your end of the bargain. If you've opted for natural consequences, then you must stay out of it. If you've included specific consequences in the contract, be prepared to keep your end of the bargain or the contract becomes meaningless.

Variations on the Contract:

For a younger child, cleaning a room may be daunting and as such, they may not be able to keep their commitment. So you can just have them put all their laundry in the basket on a Saturday morning or they could put away their books. An older child could actually do his or her laundry and see the entire process through every weekend. As I've mentioned before, your kids might surprise you!

And the contract doesn't have to be about cleaning—it can be anything you and your child agree on. It could be about homework or about committing to a particular healthy habit. The main idea of this exercise is to show kids what it means to commit to something and that there are consequences—natural or otherwise—when they don't keep their commitments.

One-Time Exercise: Our Commitment to the Environment

At the end of the month, take one day and specifically focus on everything you can do as a family to care for the environment. We chose to focus on the environment because this issue is especially important to my son, but your family can focus on any issue that is important to you.

If you choose to focus on the environment, sit down together and come up with a list of things you can do as a family that impacts the environment in a positive way. On that very day, start to implement the guidelines on your list. For instance, turn the water off when you brush your teeth, use only stainless steel bottles for water, turn off the lights when you leave the room, and maybe even plant a tree in your yard. In other words, dedicate a whole day to showing your commitment to something you believe in. Of course, the changes you make are meant to go beyond that day—but this is a great time to start living your commitment. In my house, this one day in which we committed ourselves to making positive changes for our planet has changed the way we live. A commitment can do that.

Through this exercise, you can show your children that believing in something and committing to it can have an impact. They can clearly see whether we keep the commitment or not, so if we want to impress upon them how important keeping commitments are, we really have to live this every day. It's a commitment you make as a family.

Variations on Our Commitment to the Environment:

Your family may already be living an environmentally friendly lifestyle or have another cause about which you are passionate. So making another idea the focus of this once-a-month exercise might work better for you. You may decide to spend a day with your whole family instead—no checking e-mails, no phone calls to your office, just family time. This day should be a true Family Day where you eat every meal together and have some fun. You can go miniature golfing, to an amusement park, a water park, hiking, swimming, skiing, snowboarding, to a museum—anything that the whole family would enjoy. This day can build on what you explored in Sense of Joy Month and might become a regular event in your lives

Or make a commitment as a family to being physically fit. Find a way to incorporate physical exercise into your lives regularly and do it together. Take a walk every night through your neighborhood. It will be a great way to connect as a family and to get—and stay—in shape. The main point of the exercise is that you do this once together as a family at the end of this month and then commit to make this—whatever it is—an ongoing part of your family life.

Staying Power

Our children are now very aware of what it means to make and then keep a commitment. Just the other day, my daughter, who loves to draw pictures, insisted on using both sides of the paper to help the Earth. That may be a small thing, but she used to use a ton of paper! That's a significant act for a second grader. And my son's plant is still thriving. Unfortunately, my daughter chose an orchid as her plant and it turned out to be pretty high maintenance. Sadly, it is no longer with us. Keep that in mind when doing that exercise. Choose wisely!

After this month is over, you can reinforce the lessons of commitment with your children not only by continuing to keep your own commitments, but also by letting your kids keep theirs without your help. It's so important to allow your children the freedom to succeed or fail on their own. As parents, we need to start to let go, little by little, as kids are ready to take on more responsibilities in their lives. As they make and keep their own commitments, it can feel like that is just one more thing that helps them move past relying on you. And that hurts a bit sometimes. I feel that myself. But we have to see that as a good thing. The older our kids get, the more we want them to be responsible for themselves. Hold on to the lessons of this month and keep them in mind as your kids have opportunities to step up and honor their own commitments—by themselves.

Month Nine

LIFELONG LEARNING

Always being open to what life can teach you

From our earliest moments, learning is a part of life. Our babies learn to trust us, and we learn how to feed them, bathe them, and burp them. As time goes on, the learning continues. Toddlers learn to walk and reach out their hands to us to catch them when they are afraid they might fall. Moms and dads learn how to let go, just a little, with every new step they take. Learning is everywhere. And it doesn't stop in childhood. At least it shouldn't.

Lifelong learning motivates us to try new things and revel in our efforts long after those first early steps. As parents, you can teach your children to love learning and to relish new experiences their whole lives as you learn right along with them. As a matter of fact, children teach parents some of the most profound things we will ever learn. During this month, the focus will be on teaching your children that learning isn't confined to school buildings, as blessed as they are to have such opportunities. Life is their classroom if they are taught to be open to learning.

All my life I have been a passionate learner. This is due in large part to my mother who respected and encouraged my tendency to be curious about things. Because she loves learning as much as I do, and is a teacher by profession, she always looked for ways to create opportunities for learning. I can remember many family meals when my mom would be giving a history lesson, using strategically placed vegetables to drive home her point. "Okay, these are the Huns" she would say, as she slid the bowl of mashed potatoes menacingly across the table in an aggressive offense against the peas, who were clearly doomed! Learning was everywhere for me, and I reveled in it.

My passion for learning is so much a part of me that I couldn't miss out on sharing this cherished value with my children. So in my family, we like to take the month of September, when our kids are starting a new school year, to focus on lifelong learning. You might be wondering why we don't call it "Education Month." Well, we considered that. But we didn't want our children to only associate learning with formal education, as important as that is to us. We want to encourage them to embrace lifelong learning, both in terms of school, and in the opportunities for learning in their everyday lives.

Month Nine

The way I see it, as long as you are open to new experiences and have the willingness to make mistakes and even fail, then you will never stop learning.

The idea of kids failing at something may seem out of place in our competitive society. We talked about this in Self-Respect Month and it naturally comes up again this month. I think it's important because the whole concept of learning involves being exposed to new things—things we probably won't be good at right off the bat *because* they are new to us. During Lifelong Learning Month, really encourage your kids to have fun with the *process* of learning: being introduced to something new, listening to someone who knows more about the topic at hand, or reading about it, and then trying it for themselves. And if they want to be proficient at something, then it's also going to take practice, and more practice.

Let's use bowling as an example. A child, or most adults for that matter, don't typically bowl strikes their first time in a bowling alley. Some people never get there. But enough about me. Most kids will throw numerous gutter balls, maybe even a few balls backward or down the lane next to them. Yikes! That's learning, and we should all encourage our kids to have fun with it and to embrace and learn from their mistakes, hopefully, without harming anyone!

Sure, that moment when your child gets a strike, or even knocks down his first pin, is pretty awesome. But that probably happened because he started to listen to a more experienced bowler's advice about how to adjust his stance and the way he released the ball. Or maybe he simply observed a good bowler throw a few strikes and tried to copy what he saw. And he started to notice that as he got used to it, with practice, he got a little better, though that's not always the case. Even if a child, or an adult, doesn't get much better at a particular skill with practice, that's okay too. The point is to be willing to try new things and be open to learning.

Of course, sometimes you will recognize that your child has a special talent or passion for what they've just started learning. Encourage your children to pursue their passions more seriously at that point, and recognize that if they have a genuine talent or passion for something, it will take discipline and commitment in order to achieve any level of true proficiency. Build on what your family has learned in previous months, especially during Commitment Month. But for now, during this particular month, one of the primary goals is to instill a love of learning in your children. Start with the daily exercise, which pulls learning outside the classroom and makes it into an everyday happening that is fun and educational at the same time.

Supplies for This Month's Exercises:

- For both the daily and end-of-the-month exercise, you'll need at least thirty sheets of loose-leaf paper and one inexpensive three-ring binder.

Daily Exercise: Question of the Day

At the beginning of this month, you and your spouse or partner should sit down and come up with thirty questions designed to inspire your children to learn something new. Write down all the questions on loose-leaf pieces of paper and tuck them away so the kids can't peek at upcoming questions. Each morning, put the question of the day in a binder the kids can easily access. Typically, the questions aren't about things they would have learned in school, although they can certainly be about science, history, music, or other school subjects. However, be careful that these questions don't feel like an extension of school, in addition to their everyday homework. The idea is to make it fun and interesting, so that they'll look forward to it every day.

One morning, the entry in the binder might be "*Twinkle, Twinkle Little Star* has five verses, though most people are familiar with only the first. Learn one of the other verses and sing it for your family." Or, "What is interesting about Fibonacci numbers?" If your kids love animals like my daughter does, one day the question might be, "What can you tell me about a bilby?" My children are five years apart so we thought about using two sets of questions, one for each level. But that didn't go over well with my daughter, who likes to keep up with her big brother. If there is an age and/or learning gap between your children, try using one set of questions and encouraging the kids to answer the question in their own way. If you ask for three pieces of information about a topic, then perhaps your younger child only needs to provide one or two.

In order to make the most of the exercise and learning experience, stay away from questions that only have one possible answer. For instance, don't use questions like "What is the capital city of Angola?" because there's only one answer to that and that would be Luanda. The learning would pretty much end there and the goal is not for your kids to look up a fact, write it down, and be done with it. Try to ask them questions that have more than one answer, so that they actually have to read about a subject. For example, if your kids love playing with hula-hoops, ask them about the history of the hula-hoop, and have them tell you two or three things they have learned about it. Another question might be "How do you do the waltz? Learn the basic steps." Or, "What are the first seven musical notes in "Rudolph the Red Nosed Reindeer"? Supervise them on the computer if they want to look up information, or consider buying a children's encyclopedia or borrowing one from the library. Once in a while, you may ask them their opinion on something so that they feel encouraged to *have* an opinion on matters of education and learning. Every day, each child writes down what he or she has learned about the day's subject on a page in the binder, which then becomes a little book of knowledge the whole family can use together. We used just one page for each day, and in our case, both kids wrote their answers on that same page. Feel free to use more pages if that works better for your family.

Here are some suggestions for questions I used with my kids. Questions for younger children follow this list.

- What can you tell me about the phonograph?
- What sports figure described himself as "The Luckiest Man on the Face of the Earth"? Why?
- When a mama beluga whale gives birth, why is it best that her calf is born tail first?
- What can you tell me about the Rosetta Stone?
- In your opinion, what is the most important invention in history?
- How do you do the cha-cha? Be prepared to do the basic steps.
- What is the moral of Aesop's fable "The Lion and the Mouse"?
- What did Beulah Henry do that changed the world?

- What three things can you learn about the wild horses of Shackleford Banks?
- Who was Jackson Pollack? Print out an example of his work or create a piece inspired by his work.
- What type of things is henna used for?
- Learn a short poem and be prepared to recite it out loud.
- What's the most well-known landmark in your town or city? Why?
- What's the science behind microwave popcorn?
- What are noctilucent clouds?
- What is a "MacGuffin" according to Alfred Hitchcock?
- How did your town or city get its name?
- Why do schools typically start by September and finish sometime in June?
- What is unusual about how the knight moves in chess?
- What's the farthest place on the Earth from where you are now?
- Find out what pointillism is and make your own creation using this technique.
- What can dolphins figure out using echolocation?
- How are rainbows formed?
- What are the origins of pizza?

Many of the questions above may work for a younger child, but some of them may be too complex. This exercise isn't meant to intimidate younger children, so if needed, use simpler questions for them. If they need your help to figure out how to find the answers, you can certainly offer guidance on the process. But encourage them to do as much as they can on their own.

Questions for Children in the Five-to-Seven Age Group

- How do you count to ten in a language other than English?
- How is chocolate made?
- Where does the teddy bear get his name?
- What does Charlotte do for Wilber in the book Charlotte's Web?
- In what section of an orchestra is the tuba and what does it sound like?
- What is Dr. Martin Luther King's most famous line?
- What game is played on the floor with people as game pieces?
- What does a philanthropist do?
- Draw a picture of a menorah, a kinara, or an Advent wreath with candles—make sure it is something that is not used in your religious tradition—and write down something you learned about it.
- What city in the United States holds the record for the most snow in one day and how much snow did they get?

I know you are busy parents, so don't worry about looking up all the answers to the provided questions. I'll post the answers on my website *www.maryodonohue.com*.

Variations on Question of the Day:

You may wish to focus on a particular category for this exercise, like music, art, or science. You could also choose world cultures to build on the lessons from Respect for Others Month. Or you may decide to focus on something that is very important to you as a parent, and day-by-day help your children explore and learn about that topic. It could be your profession, or a hobby you love, like photography, gardening, fishing, or quilting. That way, your children will also get to know more about you as a three-dimensional person with skills and interests of your own, and not just as a mom or dad. As the month progresses, your kids will be immersed in a new topic and they might get some insight as to why it means something to you. Maybe they will even embrace it as a hobby, and you'll share that with them as they grow up.

You could even decide to learn a new sport with your entire family or teach your kids a sport you already play. Your daily questions could involve sports terms and skills related to the sport you've chosen. If your children love to read, or you want to promote a love of reading with them, you might even focus all of the daily questions on a particular book of your own choosing. You can read a few paragraphs or a chapter each night with your kids, and have them read aloud as well. Then base your daily questions on the material you read the night before. Many chapter books already have a list of questions at the end of the book, which makes it easier. Again, this could be something that builds on a value your family has already focused on, like commitment, self-respect, or gratitude. If the books are short, you could even read one book a week and use four books as your source for the daily questions. Whatever works for you and your family, as long as your children are answering one question a day throughout this month.

Amy experienced Lifelong Learning Month with her two daughters, ages six and nine, and found a great way to do this exercise. She and her daughters found opportunities to learn with everyday situations. One night she served a dish her girls had never tried before—roasted eggplant. Her girls were quite curious about this new food and they had all kinds of questions. What was it? Where does it come from? Does it come in other colors? Amy made that the focus for learning that day and she and the girls went online, did research and created a document so they would remember what they had learned. They even asked Amy to make ratatouille!

Because education is so important, and because it is something that I don't ever want my children to take for granted, we add one more layer to this exercise in the form of a game. Well, actually, it's more like a game show. That's where the binder will come in very handy. Stay tuned . . . the game show comes at the end of the month!

Weekly Exercise: You Be the Teacher

Every weekend during the month, each child in the family must teach something they know—a particular skill they have, or just something they are good at—to someone else in the family. They can teach it to their sibling or to a parent. Kids are so used to being "learners" both at home and at school, that they don't often get a chance to be the one doing the teaching. This exercise gives them the chance to be on that side of the learning equation.

They can teach a song or dance, explain a card game or a board game to someone who has never played before, or even teach something they've learned at school. It can be anything as long as it's positive and is something new to the person being taught. And if a child is teaching something to a younger sibling, it should be appropriate for the child's age and comfort levels. For instance, your son may be learning about insects in science class, but the topic may be frightening to his younger sister. This exercise is not meant to be used to torture little brothers and sisters! So make sure the children run the topic by a parent first. You may also want to hang around nearby not only to make sure the lesson is progressing, but also because seeing your kids interact like this is really enjoyable.

For this exercise, my daughter, who loves gymnastics, decided to teach her brother how to do a new gymnastics move she was really good at. He wasn't quite able to do the move, but he sure tried. And the best part about it was that my daughter genuinely did her best to teach him, and they laughed their way through it. For her, as a little sister, it was awesome to be the one who had mastered something her big brother couldn't do. That gave my son a new perspective on his little sister, and helped him to realize that she knows things he doesn't. That's a great building block for respect, so it harkens back to the lessons learned in Respect for Others Month. One of the things my son is good at is magic, and he choose to teach a magic trick to his sister. Each of them performed the trick for me and I was really impressed!

One of the reasons this exercise works is that a lot of the interaction between siblings can be negative or competitive. But not in this case. This exercise fosters respect and positive interactions between siblings. The kids see that their brother or sister is good at something they're not good at, and is willing to teach them. And the child who is in the role of teacher gets to be looked up to by their sibling. It is also special when they teach something to a grownup in the family. Maybe for the first time in their lives, the children are showing a grownup how to do something. And they really enjoy the role-reversal. Not only is it fun for the children and grownups, but it can also go a long way toward building on the lessons you focused on in Self-Respect Month.

Variations on You Be the Teacher:

If your kids can't think of anything they feel confident teaching to another family member, try a sort of "round robin" approach. So, using my family as an example, it would work like this. Let's say I remember a fun jump rope game from my childhood. I might take my son outside and teach the game to him. Then we invite my daughter out, and my son has to teach it to her. Last, but not least, my husband comes outside and my daughter teaches him the game. This approach can work well for shy children too, because they aren't the center of attention as they try to teach a new skill to a sibling or parent. Another benefit is that this gets the whole family involved at the same time, so it fosters togetherness. And if you do it this way, each child gets to learn something new and then teach it to someone else.

Another approach would be to write down on index cards several things that your children enjoy—this could even be playing video games or with a favorite toy—and once a week, choose an index card at random for each child. Then they must teach that skill, like how to play that cool video game, to their sibling(s) or to Mom or Dad. The point of this exercise is to give kids an opportunity to teach, so whether it's geometry concepts, chess, or the finer points of handheld gaming doesn't really matter. The goal is for kids to understand that teaching isn't necessarily easy but

Month Nine

it is rewarding. This exercise gives kids a chance to see what their teachers (and you!) go through, and will truly help them appreciate the challenges of teaching.

One-Time Exercise: Earning for Learning

This month culminates with your very own game show. Encourage your kids to study the little book of knowledge they have put together because they will be quizzed on the information they have learned. The questions of the day will be the basis for the game show and each child can earn $1 or any amount that works for you for every correct answer they give. This money isn't given to them so they can go out and buy a new video game or toy. This month is about the importance of learning and education, after all. And many kids, mine included, often take their formal education for granted, complaining about hard tests and too much homework. Meanwhile, there are many children around the world who would dearly love to attend school but their families simply cannot afford it or they don't have a school to go to. Those children have dreams just like your kids and mine—dreams to be a doctor, a teacher, or an astronaut, but without education, those dreams are unachievable.

It's important for children to realize how fortunate they are to be *burdened* with homework and history tests. So, at the end of the game show, the kids each take the money they have earned and use it to pay for education for a child living in poverty. You can do this through a number of charities—the one we choose is called the Girl's Global Education Fund (*www .ggef.org*), an organization that sends girls to school who would otherwise be unable to get an education. This is the charity we have selected, but take the time to research this charity and others and choose the one that is the best fit for your family. The important thing is that by helping a child they'll never meet go to school, your kids can make an enormous impact on that child's future.

This is the only exercise that may cost a significant amount of money, roughly $40–$80 per child, but it doesn't have to cost much at all. What's nice is that this exercise builds on the value of compassion and shows children that they can make a significant difference in the life of another child their age.

Variations on Earning for Learning:

This exercise is not about spending a lot of money, so you can have the kids play for dimes or quarters—whatever is comfortable for your family. With the money raised, you can buy books, school supplies, or a backpack for a child in your community—or halfway around the world. It doesn't matter, as long as the money raised goes to help another child in the pursuit of a formal education. This is very empowering for the children who do the exercise and helps them see that education is not free and shouldn't be taken for granted.

Staying Power

Because of the exercises and the message of this month, you may see interesting and unexpected benefits, such as increased patience, in your children. For some kids, teaching someone fosters patience! That's been a revelation for our children, although my husband and I had figured that one out for ourselves after having children. And both kids have more empathy for their teachers, and understand how difficult it can be to try to teach a roomful of children, after they themselves have taken a hand at teaching. You may see improvements in yourself and your partner as well. My husband sees the importance of learning more than ever before. He takes the time for teaching moments, especially with Grace, and she encourages him to ask her harder questions. She likes to be challenged!

You can keep the learning going for your family as well. I encourage you to be open to the many possibilities for learning in everyday life, like Amy who found an opportunity for her daughters to learn just by making a new dish for dinner. And allow your children to teach you things—whether they have discovered something about history in school or picked up a fascinating fact on their favorite cartoon. Encourage their enthusiasm about learning on trips to museums, visits to the zoo, or even right in your own backyard. Look for opportunities to discover things together as a family so you can show your children that lifelong learning can and should be a part of their whole lives.

Month Ten

INNER STRENGTH

Being able to cope when the going gets tough

There's something about being a parent—maybe it's the fact that you love your children so immensely—that brings out your inner strength. Some of you may have faced times when your children were very sick and you didn't think you had the strength to go in their hospital room and be there for them. But you did it somehow, because that's what they needed from you. Moms and dads may not be superheroes, but sometimes as a parent, you have to muster up courage you didn't know you had because that's what your child needs.

This month is about equipping your child with that same necessary inner strength. Because there will be times, as much as you hate to think about it, when your child will face hardships. At some point in our lives, all of us go through painful times. Instead of just trying to protect your children from all the bad stuff out there, you will be glad you have also enabled them to face it on their own someday by teaching them about inner strength.

I remember when my son was just a baby. I was the stereotypical overprotective mom. You know—on hot summer days I would make sure he had on gobs of sunscreen, a sun hat, a T-shirt to cover his shoulders and yes, even an umbrella to keep him in the shade. Then in the winter I dressed him so warmly he could barely walk. Then if he fell, it was okay—his layers of clothing would easily cushion his fall. Not that I would let him fall, mind you. I was always right there holding out a steady hand in case he faltered. I was going to make sure that no one or nothing ever hurt my sweet boy. You might be conjuring up an image of those helicopter moms I've mentioned before—the ones who hover around their older children—but they had nothing on me. I was like a full-on squadron of copters on constant alert.

Then one day it happened. Somehow, somebody got through my clearly inadequate defenses and made my little boy sad—broke his heart in fact. And he wasn't even two years old. It all started out quite happily. We had decided to get a dog and had chosen the sweetest little collie puppy you can imagine. We named him Rory, and my son was absolutely delighted and quickly became very close to his new puppy. Sadly, just three weeks after we brought Rory home from the breeder, he died. The vet told us that our puppy had not been properly cared for by the inexperienced or unscrupulous breeder.

And I'm not going to lie to you. My son did suffer. He was pretty sad for a few days on and off. But, at less than two years old, he was really just a baby. He adjusted much better than I had thought he would. I wish I could say I learned to ease up a bit, and let my child venture off into the world a little more on his own. But I'm afraid I actually got worse. I vowed to protect him much better this time, so I battened down the hatches and went into overprotective mommy overdrive.

And you know something? It was the wrong thing to do. Back in those days though, I was pretty new to the mom thing. I was a rookie, and I was overcompensating. It took a few years and a second child to start to turn me around. In time, I began to give my kids room to deal with their own disappointments. And that's a good thing. After all, if our kids learn to cope with little bumps in the road as they grow up, they will surely be better prepared for the bigger bumps they will inevitably face. Kids are often stronger than we think they are, if we only give them a chance to show it. And that's the point of this whole month. Though you may not be able to give your children inner strength—you can teach them how important it is, and help them develop and value the strength they already have.

Having true inner strength isn't reserved for superheroes, or just for tragedies. Like compassion, inner strength is an every-day value. It's something all of us can possess. In fact, it's one of the quietest of values. You may not notice it when you see it, but it's there. It's the kind of thing you see in a little girl when a classmate has hurt her feelings, but she gets up the next day, goes back to school, and faces the problem. Or when a young boy has an illness and does what needs to be done to get better—swallowing icky-tasting medicine and changing his diet, even though that may not be easy. He does it and gets on with it. That's everyday courage and it's all around us.

What's Strength Got to Do with It?

It may be difficult for a child to recognize inner strength or understand what it is. So, try to make the concept of inner strength as concrete as possible to your children. I like to use an analogy based on something my kids are both familiar with from science class. They've learned about warm-blooded animals like dogs and birds, whose body temperatures are regulated internally and cold-blooded animals like frogs and snakes, who are unable to regulate their body temperatures internally so they take on the temperature of their surroundings. This is a great example of how inner strength works. If a person does not have inner strength, he is only happy when things are going well in his life. But when circumstances change and things take a turn for the worse, he is depressed and afraid. But picture a person with inner strength. Certainly, she is affected by sad or happy events in her life, but she doesn't let outside influences and circumstances control her. She has strength and resilience no matter what is happening in her world. As it turns out, the idea of being more like a puppy and less like a toad appeals to my seven-year-old daughter! This simple example has really helped both of my kids understand and internalize the idea of what it means to have inner strength. I think it will resonate with your children, too.

As your kids start to understand what it means to be emotionally strong, also explore the idea of emotional weakness.

During this month, talk to them about the erroneous concept that expressing emotions, especially by crying, is in some way a sign of weakness—when in fact, just the opposite is true. Encourage your children—whether they are boys or girls—to feel safe to honestly express their feelings, even if it means crying or getting upset. We all know people who bottle up their emotions. Then that straw that breaks the camel's back comes around and all of a sudden, a rush of emotions comes pouring out, and it's typically a very exaggerated response to whatever just happened. I imagine you don't want your children getting into this habit. So encourage them as much as possible to have an appropriate response when they are upset.

That means showing sadness, anger, or frustration in a way that allows kids to express what they are feeling without being hurtful. Now, of course this doesn't always happen. Emotions by their very nature can be hard to control. Give kids a basic sense of how to handle themselves by telling them it's okay to feel those emotions and to express them, but it's not okay to use any emotion as an excuse to hurt someone else's feelings. Teach them that when someone is crying or expressing anger in an appropriate way, they should do their best to listen and respond thoughtfully. That means if your ten-year-old son is crying because he didn't make the soccer team, his siblings are not supposed to make fun of him. Instead, they are encouraged to draw from what they've already learned, such as compassion and respect for others, to help their sibling.

Let your children know that there will be times when they may feel overwhelmed and unsure of what to do. When kids are in these situations, it's important that they know how to reach out for help. By teaching them how important it is to have inner strength, you are not saying they will be like rocks that can withstand every hardship. Hey, even rocks wear down over time. There will be times when, even armed with inner strength and courage, our children will feel like they are sinking. So during those times, encourage them to have the strength to reach out beyond themselves for help to trusted family members, friends, members of the clergy, or therapists and physicians if needed. Just like with expressing emotions, you never want them to think of seeking help as a sign of weakness, but rather as a sign of strength. Even the strongest among us needs help sometimes.

One of the goals of Inner Strength Month is to teach kids about being resilient, so they will be able to bounce back after an embarrassing misstep or even a failure. It's important for kids to understand that these things are not the end of the world, though to them it may seem like it at the time. As parents, we should do our best to teach our kids what it means to be strong and then try to go even deeper, by teaching them about courage. Just as in previous months, you can build on what the family has already learned, especially the lessons on self-respect and seeing themselves as capable, self-confident people. Your kids can learn these lessons through the exercises for this month.

Supplies for This Month's Exercises:

- A dry erase board
- Dry erase markers
- A clear glass vase and pitcher of water. If you like, food coloring can be used to dye the water.

Daily Exercise: Inner Strength Word of the Day

For the daily exercise this month, start by introducing words that help children understand the many facets of having true inner strength—things like adaptability, tenacity, and fortitude. Each morning, write the word on a large dry erase board in your kitchen or wherever your family gathers.

Ask the kids to look up the definitions of the words or offer suggestions on what they think the words mean. It will only take a few minutes, and you can do this at the breakfast table or another time of day that is convenient for the family. Write the definitions each day and either erase it the next day, or add to it if there is room.

Every day as the month goes along, explain to your kids that these words demonstrate ways in which they can express their own inner strength. This helps your children see that this value isn't necessarily about being tough. It can also mean using humor or patience to get through difficult times and to cope with the daily stresses of life. Ask that the entire family keep the word in mind as each of you go through your day.

For instance, if the word of the day is "independence," talk about what that means—the ability to be self-reliant, to handle things on their own. Explain to your kids that they should develop this quality over time and that the degree of independence they display should be age appropriate. Then, give them the opportunity to show their independence that day. Maybe instead of opening the pickle jar for your son, let him figure out how to do it on his own. Or if your spouse or partner is tempted to swoop in and solve a problem your daughter is having, allow her the time and space to figure it out on her own. It may not have been the solution you would have thought of, but it's her challenge.

At the end of the day, ask your kids if the word of the day was something that inspired them that day, and if so, how? If not, maybe they could think of a way they could use that quality of inner strength in their lives. Mind you, we can't expect that every day the word will be lived per se. The goal is that your entire family will be more aware of the myriad tools of inner strength that are available to each of you, and you'll be inspired to use these tools as you need them.

This exercise is a great way to see how your kids are developing their inner strength in ways you may not have thought of. For instance, my son pointed out that he's learned a lot about one of our words of the day—determination—just by playing video games. He asked me if I'd ever heard him say, "I'll never get past this level! This is so hard!" while playing a video game. Sure, I had—lots of times. Then he asked me if I'd ever heard him say, "I give up!" while playing a game. As a matter of fact, I hadn't. "That's because video games can teach determination. They teach you to always keep trying," he said. Who knew?

Examples of Inner Strength Words or Phrases of the Day:

- Resilience
- Resourcefulness
- Peace of mind
- Courage
- Perspective
- Gutsiness
- Resolve

- Conviction
- Steadiness
- Diligence
- Discipline
- Self-Control
- Grit
- Steadfast
- Perseverance
- Backbone
- Endure
- Confide
- Character
- Indomitable
- Overcome
- Self-Awareness
- Power

Katie, a mom who spent a month focusing on Inner Strength with her fourteen-year-old daughter and nine year old son, posted their daily words on the door of their fridge. Her daughter really responded to the word "security" and felt that sometimes kids her age are mean because they are insecure. Katie's son was especially inspired by the word "nurturing" because he said it makes him feel strong to comfort others.

Variations on the Inner Strength Word of the Day:

You may prefer to keep a record of what has been learned throughout the month. To do so, you can create an "Inner Strength Word of the Day" document on your computer or in a simple notebook and keep track of the definitions for each word. At the end of the month, you'll have a list of the words and definitions to refer back to at any time, or you can print out the document, or simply send it to your family members if you all have e-mail.

If your kids are artistic, another option is to encourage them to draw a picture of what the word means to them each day. It doesn't have to take more than a few minutes. Maybe they do it after school, and if they have been able to utilize the word of the day to express their inner strength, they could even write a few lines saying how they did it. Make it an ongoing comic strip if you or someone in your family has that talent. The point is to make an impression on your kids so they will remember the tools they have to help them be strong throughout their lives. Do this exercise in any way that you feel will be most memorable to your kids.

Weekly Exercise: Three Reasons

The goal of the weekly exercise is to help your children understand that they have a choice about how to react to difficult events and circumstances. But even as adults, it can be hard to know what to do in a particular situation. Often we as parents don't realize the tremendous pressure our children can be under from their peers. So for this exercise, try out some situations your children may encounter in their everyday lives. Help them figure out what to do by giving them specific ways they can stand up to other kids who are pressuring them to do things they're not comfortable with, or things they know are wrong, and might even be dangerous.

For instance, if you have a son in junior high school, you might imagine a situation in which a classmate approaches your son and suggests that he smoke a cigarette to be part of the "in" crowd. Talk about what he thinks he would do if that situation happened today. He might say that he would not know what to say, or might feel embarrassed especially if there were a large group of boys around. So help him have three reasons why he shouldn't smoke cigarettes and show him how to use his inner strength to deflect the peer pressure in that situation.

When we did this exercise in my house, one of the things we asked our son was if he saw himself being comfortable smoking cigarettes. He didn't, so we pointed out that it isn't who he is. It just isn't him. We always encourage our kids to "know who they are" throughout this year of values. So he could simply say to the kids "Smoking—it's just not me." Reason two would be that it is considered to be unhealthy, and reason three could be that it costs a lot of money and he'd rather spend what little money he has on video games. To him, that's a lot more fun and a lot cooler than smoking. These three reasons help him clarify in his own mind why smoking doesn't appeal to him. So when there is peer pressure to smoke, he is prepared with reasons he himself believes in instead of just parroting what we as his parents have said.

For younger children, the issues may be different. Maybe a friend of your six-year-old daughter is making fun of a classmate. That is peer pressure as well because your daughter may feel that unless she goes along with the taunting, she may be next in line. Talk to her about knowing who she is and how important that is, just as you would do with your older children. Instead of asking a younger child what she would say in that situation, ask her, "Do you see yourself as the sort of person who would make fun of someone?" Inevitably, she'll say "no." But did she sit idly by as other kids made fun of another child? If so, help her to understand that it's also wrong to do that. Ask her to think about having inner strength and then talk about ways to respond to the situation that show her strength.

You can use the three-reason method here, too. Reason one might be that your child does not see herself as the kind of person who would make fun of another child—it's just not who she is, or wants to be. Reason two might be that it's wrong to try to hurt someone's feelings, and reason three could be that she values kindness and therefore she's not going to participate in taunting someone else. Maybe she can even take it a step further and play with the other child. The point of this exercise is to come up with situations your kids might actually see themselves in and help them to know specifically what to do and why.

This exercise gives your children opportunities to explore what they believe in. Encourage them to express those beliefs with confidence. Oftentimes when children are being pressured to do something they are not comfortable with, they know in their hearts they want to say no but they don't know how to say it effectively. Your children may find themselves in a situation where they are urged by classmates to cheat on a test, or might be encouraged to repeat an inappropriate word or comment they heard from someone else. They may even feel pressured by siblings to do things they aren't comfortable with like sneaking out of bed to play games or taking things that don't belong to them. These are the types of situations you can break down and explore to help your kids to find three reasons to stand up for what they feel is the right thing to do. Having this tool will help them find and express their inner strength.

Variations on Three Reasons:

If you don't feel that peer pressure is an issue for your child, then you might prefer to focus on issues that come up, such as feeling worried about getting into the high school of their choice, or in families affected by divorce, how they can handle living in two households. You can sit down with your kids and instead of coming up with three reasons, come up with three things that will help them cope with their particular worry. In the case of living in two homes, maybe they would feel better if they had a written schedule to remind them of where they will be and when. They may also want both parents at their dance recitals, or basketball games to help them feel a sense of normalcy. The third thing could be giving them the option of joining a support group for children of divorce where they could feel safe to talk openly about their feelings. Whatever the problem is, sitting down with them and working out three things to help them feel stronger emotionally can mean a lot.

One-Time Exercise: The Reservoir of Inner Strength

Most parents would agree that our reserves of inner strength are at their greatest when we take care of ourselves and do things that help keep us emotionally and physically strong and healthy. The purpose of this last exercise is to remind your kids that it's possible to burn through their inner strength reserves when times get very tough or even when the day-to-day stress of life gets to be too much for them. You want them to understand there are many ways to fill up that reservoir, so to speak.

For this exercise, sit down with your kids and take out a large clear vase. Have a pitcher full of water next to the vase and add a little green or blue food coloring to make the exercise more visual, and therefore more memorable. Ask the kids to think of things that will keep their reservoir of inner strength filled and ready for them when they need it. Some things we've come up with in my house are getting a good night's sleep, playing with a pet, and going sledding.

Discuss how each of these things helps them feels relaxed and replenished, and as you talk about each one, have them pour a little bit of water from the pitcher into the clear vase. Come up with several more and when the vase is about a third full, stop for a moment. At that point, you should come up with something that is stressful or upsetting that might happen in their lives, such as losing their homework or finding out a friend is moving away, and pour out some of the water into the sink. Show them that going through a stressful or upsetting time, or even day after day of minor difficulties, is like using up some of their reserve inner strength. So what do we do to replenish it?

Think of more ways to fill the vase with water as you list other ways to help yourselves be, and stay, strong. Talking to a friend, spending time on a relaxing hobby, taking a nice warm bath, or spending time in nature can be very restorative, and all of these can be very important ways to keep your inner strength reserves full. This is a lesson for grownups too, especially parents. Too often, we just keep going and going until we fall down, not ever really taking the time to take care of ourselves. But if we don't keep our inner strength reserves full, it ends up affecting us, and our families, in a negative way. So you can take a lesson from this exercise just like your kids do.

Once you fill up the vase, you are done with the exercise, but you should write down the various positive things you have come up with and post them in your house so you can all be reminded of ways to nurture your inner strength. Try to make sure that you each do at least one of these things every day.

Other Ideas for Ways to Keep Your Inner Strength Reserves Full:

- Play
- Take a short nap
- Make something with your own hands
- Sit down, put your feet up, and listen to soothing music
- Plant flowers in your garden
- Go for a walk with your family
- Immerse yourself in a happy book
- Cuddle up and watch a movie that makes you laugh
- Do something you love every day
- Go on a picnic
- Take up tai chi or yoga with the whole family
- Be a positive thinker
- Choose a hobby and do it often—like quilting, painting, or learning to play a musical instrument
- Eat fresh fruits and vegetables
- Do a crossword or Sudoku puzzle

- Do what you're doing when you're doing it, instead of trying to do too many things at the same time
- Pray or meditate
- Eat dinner with your family without phones, TV, or any electronics
- Journal
- Dance
- Take ten minutes and just watch the birds outside your window
- Play a board game with someone in your family
- Keep a scrapbook
- Sing your favorite song
- Bake a favorite recipe with your family
- Do a jigsaw puzzle
- Write a poem or story
- Go for a bicycle ride

Variations on the Reservoir of Inner Strength:

If you don't want to use the vase with water example that we use in my house, instead just talk with your kids about ways to keep their inner strength reservoirs full. Have them draw a picture of where they feel their inner strength reservoir is at the moment. What ideas do they have to fill it? Look at the list above and do one or more of the activities with your kids at the end of this month. Maybe your whole family can decide to take a stroll around the block together every evening after dinner. If your family didn't decide to take up walking back in Commitment Month, this may be a good time to revisit that idea. It will ease your individual and collective stress, replenish your inner strength reserves, and keep you close as a family.

Staying Power

After Inner Strength Month, my son took a film class with two other boys his age whom he had never met before. At lunchtime, the other boys were talking about violent movies they liked and the gory special effects they wanted to use in their film projects. I am one of those moms who is pretty wary of violent video games and movies, so my son hasn't really been exposed to violence. He told the other boys that, and when they made fun of him, he stood his ground, telling them that he doesn't like violence and didn't plan to include it in his film. He went on to tell them that he preferred family films. He offered to help them on their films except for the violent bits and in the end, they took his help and assisted on his film as well.

After this month is over, if you find your child facing an obstacle, remind them of some of the words they learned this month. Perhaps some patience and perspective can help them get through what they are dealing with. Maybe they need to talk it out to find the right way to approach the issue, by figuring out how they really feel about it. Reinforce that they have many tools at their disposal and see if finding a way to replenish their inner strength reserves would help in any way. If what they are dealing with is overwhelming, remind them that there are people who can help them, starting with you—their parent.

I know it's not always easy to help your child through a rough time. For one thing, having your son or daughter draw on their inner strength can be a painful concept to deal with as a parent. What parent wants their child to face difficult times? But try this. Imagine one of those fairy tales where the young knight or princess sets off on a journey through a dark forest where they will no doubt face ornery ogres and dastardly dragons. Well, they may have a steely sword, or a lightning-fast steed as a sidekick, but neither one of those will get them past their formidable foes. Ultimately, it's their determination, courage, resilience, and perseverance—in short, their inner strength—that they will draw on to face and overcome those obstacles. And they wouldn't be likely to succeed unless their fairy tale moms and dads had prepared them for the perils of their journeys. Would those parents have said to their young ones, "Everything will be absolutely lovely. You are the best! Have a nice trip now"? Not so much. It's more likely they would have let their kids know that the journey was not going to be easy, but that they had courage and the strength within them to overcome whatever they encountered.

Well, life is no fairy tale. The ogres and dragons our children may face will come in other forms, but will be just as challenging to overcome. Surely we can do as well as those imaginary moms and dads in the fairy tales who prepared their children for their journeys rather than shielding them from the obstacles that they would inevitably face.

As parents, you may struggle with the thought that your kids will have to go through tough times. I'm right there with you, believe me. But we do our kids no favors by sending them out into the world unprepared and vulnerable. Life is hard sometimes, and it is even harder for those people who are completely unprepared. By spending a month teaching your children about the importance of inner strength, you will be giving them tools they can use as they embark on their journeys. And it doesn't mean they'll never need you. What is does mean is that you will be raising strong, independent children who will be able to make their own way in the world. And that's better than a fairy tale any day.

Month Eleven

SPIRITUALITY

Feeling a sacred connection to a higher power

Teaching your children about spirituality can be very challenging, as being spiritual is a very personal experience. At the same time, a child enters our life almost as a kind of ethereal being. Children seem closer to the mystery of being spiritual than many of us are as adults. Something about the innocence of being a child connects to the divine. It isn't about organized religion, and it doesn't matter what house of worship you attend or haven't attended for years. Children seem to have an intrinsic connection to God, or the universe, or whatever you may think of as sacred, that many of us have either forgotten about or lost somehow.

This month is about recognizing and nourishing that beautiful connection in your children, and about sharing the experience of your own spirituality with them. It isn't about being without fault. No perfection here. It's about finding that deeper connection to that which you consider sacred and sharing it with your children.

One evening as I was quizzing my seventh-grade son for an upcoming social studies test, he asked me totally out of the blue, "Does Jesus really exist? Or is he just like Santa Claus, the Tooth Fairy, and the Easter Bunny?" At first, I didn't know where the question came from. Weren't we just in the middle of talking about the Spanish conquistadors? But I could tell just by looking at my son's face that this was a sincere question, maybe something he had been mulling over for quite a while. If you think about it, many of us do tell our children that there truly is a Santa Claus and we provide ample physical evidence of this every year. How about that money left under their pillows by the Tooth Fairy? And where do those Easter eggs come from anyway? When children get to an age where they start questioning whether those fictional characters really exist, it must be very confusing. Maybe the higher power you teach your children about may seem just like the other unseen "beings" who do incredibly cool things for them. And who gets top billing? For those who believe in Jesus and celebrate Christmas—think about how the message of Jesus' birth is often drowned out by Santa Claus and the commercialization surrounding the holiday. No wonder a kid gets confused!

Many children may wonder how they can ever "know" that a higher power, like God, exists. After all, most things are real and concrete to us because we experience them through our senses. To a child, being unable to see, hear, or touch God makes it hard to believe. When my daughter started wondering if God is real, I asked if she knew I loved her. She said, "Of course, I know you love me!"

"I do love you. But you can't see my love, can you? So how do you *know* I love you?" I asked.

She looked at me and said, "I just know, Mom."

Exactly. I explained to her that I believe just like love, God is real, even though we may not be able to "see" love or "see" God. I should mention that I don't personally think God is limited to being male or female. I use the terms "God, "Him," and "He" because that's what most people who believe in God are comfortable with. But to me, the mystery of God transcends things like gender. Anyway, I explained to my daughter that to me, faith is about believing in things that are not proven to you, and may never be proven until we go to heaven to be with God. I also believe that people of genuine faith don't need to "see" God or experience Him with one of their physical senses like touch or hearing. It is deeper than that—just like love.

I personally believe that it's a positive thing when children question what they've been taught about faith. Again, spirituality is a deeply personal value, and it's not something we can, or would want to, simply hand over to our children. It is something we can and do share with them, but it must also be a value they embrace sincerely if it is to have any meaning in their own lives.

Religion and Spirituality

If the belief in something other than yourself and finding peace and solace in that belief is profoundly important to you, how can you share this with your children in a way that will become meaningful to them as individuals? For one thing, you can ask yourselves the same questions we asked of ourselves—are we living our faith? Are our children participating in our spiritual practices? For many families, regularly going to a place of worship is very important. But spirituality is more than just a religious practice, or even religion itself. Spirituality is the acknowledgment that we are all connected to one another and that there is something more powerful than each of us individually. For some people that something is God, for others it is the Universe, or a collective oneness. For others, spirituality is expressed in a profound connection with nature. However you define it, these exercises will help your children get in touch with their spirituality and see it as a real part of their everyday lives.

To further what you have explored during Respect for Others Month, you may want to take your children to services of another faith this month. This fosters a deeper understanding and respect for people who practice different religions than your own. I would suggest contacting officials at the particular place of worship you want to visit and letting them know you would like to experience their service. Respectfully ask them for any suggestions to prepare for such a visit with your children.

No matter what organized religion we practice, if we as parents don't back up those weekly visits to our place of worship with genuine examples of ways to live our faith, how will our children understand what that means? If we pray for the poor once a week but our children hear us say disparaging things about people who are struggling financially, or may be homeless, what are our children to think? If we listen to a minister, imam, rabbi, priest, or guru talk about showing compassion at a religious service but then gossip about the details of a neighbor's divorce, how do our children see our true faith in action? As parents wanting to instill a genuine faith in God or a higher power in our children, our spirituality cannot just be reserved for time spent in our place of worship. We want to instill in our children a deep and profound experience of faith that is with them every day.

One of the most important things about spirituality is about being connected—not only to God or a mystical, divine presence, but also to each other. In my house, this is an important point my husband and I share with our children during Spirituality Month. We talk about ways they can feel connected to God like being compassionate, respecting themselves and others, and being joyful. In other words, just by living our values, we can feel connected with God and honor the gifts He has given all of us.

The exercises this month are designed to reinforce the idea that faith is deeply individual and that there is sacredness in everyday life. Another one of the goals of Spirituality Month is to teach your children that even during difficult, challenging times in their lives, God is with them.

There aren't necessarily any special materials needed for this month's exercises.

Daily Exercise: My Own Prayer

If you believe in the power of prayer, during Spirituality Month it is important to do your best to teach your children to pray sincerely, from their own hearts. Sometimes when a child, or an adult for that matter, says a prayer that they have learned, they treat it as rote. They just say it without feeling the emotion of the words. A prayer isn't meant to be something that you just do. It is meant to be something that you experience, an expression of your soul. And it can be that, given the proper attention and respect.

During this month, talk to your children about the beauty of prayers and encourage them to think about the words as they are praying them aloud or silently. Then, ask them to come up with a short prayer of their own. The prayer can ask for something, it can be an expression of gratitude—it can be anything, as long as it is sincere.

As always, parents should participate in the exercise as well. I suggest taking the time to write your own prayers and sharing them with your children. This may even help inspire them with their own prayer.

For some children, this process will seem very natural to them. Use your judgment on whether or not your children will need guidance with this exercise. If they do, sit down with your kids and encourage them to list some of their hopes and dreams as well as their worries and fears. This list can provide them with food for thought as they write their prayers. My seven-year-old daughter didn't know where to begin during this exercise. I asked her to list a few things she truly felt thankful for and she actually came up with quite a long list including "love, shelter, food, family, and pets."

Then I asked her to write down a few things she could use some help with in her life. This took her a while longer. I assured her that there were no wrong answers to the question as long as she was sincere. And since my daughter's prayer belongs to her alone, I will respect her privacy and not include any more specific details about what she wrote. Once she had written down a few things for the second part of the prayer, we moved on to the last part.

At this point, I asked her to list anything she hoped God would help other people with in order to reinforce the belief that praying isn't just about focusing on ourselves. This part was easier for her, and she quickly listed ways she hoped God would help people that she loved. Once her lists were complete, I asked her to go back over what she had written and create her personal three-part prayer. The basic template for this type of prayer is as follows:

Dear God (or other higher power your family believes in),
Thank you for . . .
Please help me with . . .
Also, please help (another person) with . . .
Love,
(Child's name)

Of course, your child does not need to follow this template. But first listing things, and then using the above template, might make the whole idea more comfortable for some children. My son wrote his prayer to the tune of "Twinkle, Twinkle Little Star," so he could sing it. The last two lines he wrote are "Thank you for your tender care. That is why I sing this prayer." Whatever works! The most important thing about these prayers is that they should be personal to each child and should reflect their own sense of faith and the connection they feel with the divine. If they don't feel that connection in their own hearts, consider including a request for help in that area.

Once each child has written their prayer, ask them to say it every morning before breakfast or every night before bed. They can say it more than that if they choose, but once a day will suffice.

Parents Laurie and Jesse experienced Spirituality Month with their two children. Laurie was touched to see that she didn't need to remind her twelve-year-old son to say his own prayer. She also mentioned that her five-year-old daughter's prayer included a few simple requests, one of which was that God would attend her upcoming birthday party, which makes her prayer really lovely and unique. Over the course of the month, the children may decide to add things or take things out of their prayer. It is just that—their own prayer—so let them change it if they want to. Having their very own prayer may be a small thing but it helps them to understand that their words can be sacred, and that being spiritual is a very personal experience.

Variations on Your Own Prayer:

Your child may not be comfortable with writing out a prayer. In that case, is there a word that is important to him or her, a word that could describe something they feel, or wish for, or something they need help with? If so, they can just say that word every day as many times as they like, silently or out loud. It could be "peace," "love," "thankful," "hope," or "together." Whatever the word is, if it helps your child feel more connected to God, or to whatever your family calls the divine presence in their lives, then it can be deeply spiritual. If prayer is not a part of your spiritual practice, and you feel your child would be able to be quiet and still long enough to benefit from mediation, consider trying it. The main point of the exercise is that the word, prayer, or quiet time of meditation strengthens the connection your child feels with him or herself, and with a higher power.

Weekly Exercise: Where Is God Now?

Even those who believe deeply in God have experienced very difficult times in life when they've felt abandoned by Him and found themselves asking, "Where are you now God?" This exercise is designed to help each member of the family, especially children, find God, or their higher power during those challenging times.

Start by talking to your kids and relating stories from your own lives when you have felt this way. Ask your children to share stories, if they have them, in which they have felt that God was not with them. If they have never felt abandoned, that's wonderful, and you can talk about how God has helped them in particular situations. But if they have experienced times when they wondered where God was, and why it didn't seem like He was helping them, talk about it as a family. Together, try to see where God was in those situations. Was He actually present as a gift of patience when something they desperately wanted to happen was out of reach? Was a seemingly insurmountable obstacle put in their way so that they could find God in their ability to somehow overcome it?

These things are not obvious to a child or even many adults for that matter. It's important, then, to take the time during this month to look for ways God, or another higher power, has been there for us when we may have missed that sacred presence. In my house, we typically do this exercise once every weekend and spend about ten to fifteen minutes on it, so it isn't very time consuming but it can have a significant impact on a child. As with the other discussions you have with your kids about values, make sure it's not a lecture. It's just an opportunity to look for God, or a divine presence, in unexpected places, and to open your children's minds to the possibilities within faith.

Variations on Where Is God Now?:

You may simply wish to sit down with your family and talk about where God is at that very moment. This can help everyone in the family explore the idea that there is always a spiritual connection in your lives. As you sit together, each member of the family can try to look closely at each other and think about the relationships they share. Where is God, or a sense of the divine, in those relationships, and in the people present? Does your family somehow find humor to help you get through difficult times? Is God present there? Do any of you ever feel lost or in need of help and one of the people in your family reaches out to you for support? Is God working through them? Talking about these moments can help all of you be more aware of the divine presence in the everyday moments of your lives.

One-Time Exercise: The Maze

Have you ever wanted something so badly and kept pushing and pushing to make it happen in your life in spite of the fact that it got you nowhere? I sure have. Many times. Eventually, I would realize that what I needed to do was to let go, and to surrender to what God had in mind for me. At that point, things would start to shift in a whole new direction, often the very one I had been resisting for so long. Of course, it was the direction I should have been going in all along, though that wasn't always apparent to me right away. I just had to have faith and allow myself to go in the new direction and doors would start opening for me.

Now keep in mind, I'm not saying that every time things get hard, or obstacles are thrown in your path, you should give up. Not at all. But if you get the feeling you're going nowhere, you might be right. In my experience, that's the time to step back and reassess the path you're on.

It's sort of like working your way through a maze. You can't really see where you're supposed to go and you keep running into one obstacle after another. Sometimes it gets so frustrating you just want to push through the obstacles rather than following the path that's laid out for you. That's the point of this exercise: to show your children that sometimes the thing they want most to happen in their lives isn't happening because it's not what God has in mind for them.

For this one-time exercise, ask your kids to imagine something great that they have been trying to make happen in their lives, but for some reason it hasn't worked out yet. Make sure it's something specific—like making the soccer team, being chosen as cheerleader, or getting into the school of their choice. Then, ask each of your kids to imagine that the thing they really want is possible if they are able to find their way through a kind of life-sized maze. You can do this exercise with just you and your child or as many people as are in your family. Simply have one child at a time walk through a room, or your backyard, with a particular path in mind to get from one point to another, as far away from their starting point as possible. Tell them that the end point of their path represents achieving their goal. Then, have yourself, your spouse, or partner, and all your children, stand in the way to represent obstacles. The rule is that the child going through the maze cannot push anyone—they must simply walk around any "obstacle" in their way. Do this for a few minutes, having the "obstacles" move so that they are frequently in the path of the child walking.

When the child trying to walk through the "maze" starts to get a bit frustrated, stop and tell them that sometimes God puts obstacles in our way because He's trying to get us to go in a better direction. Discuss with your children how navigating our way through life can be challenging at times. Often, it feels like we just keep hitting dead ends or somehow ending up back where we started. Sometimes life can indeed feel like a gigantic maze! From our vantage point, we can't really figure out where to go next. Sure, there's lots of trial and error, and sometimes we are able to find the right path. Other times, however, we may feel lost and unsure about how to move on in life.

Ask your kids to imagine that God has a completely different perspective on that maze. Imagine that He can look down and see the maze in its entirety. He knows what path is meant for us, and if we have faith and allow ourselves to be still and open to our deeper spirituality, then we can be guided in our lives by God. That's where faith comes in.

Variations on the Maze

If you prefer not to do a physical exercise, or if you or your child have physical limitations, then feel free to create a little maze on a piece of paper. If you are very creative and craft-oriented, you could even make a mini three-dimensional maze. Or to make it simple, just use one of those maze puzzle books or download a maze off the Internet. Sit with your children and have them work their way through the maze. Let them know that when they choose a path to go down, it may turn out to be the wrong path for them, even though it felt like the right direction. Point out to them as they find their way through the maze that sometimes God has a direction in mind for them, and if they keep the faith and are open to going in a new and different direction, that is often when they get to where they were meant to be.

Staying Power

In the car recently, as we stopped to allow an ambulance to speed by, I heard something coming from the backseat. It was my daughter, praying for the people who needed the ambulance. She does this now every time she sees an ambulance. This may seem like a small thing, but before we spent a month focusing on spirituality, I don't recall her ever even noticing when an ambulance would pass us by. Now she not only is noticing; she is praying for those inside. It is just part of her own spiritual practice now.

I want to stress one more time that this month is not about organized religion. Being part of a faith community can be a significant part of spiritual life for many people, but for others, it has no place. There is no judgment here. This month is about sharing what is most spiritual to you with your own children. Sharing those deeply held beliefs with your children can give them the framework to understand and develop their own spirituality, and it can also bring you even closer to your children. After you spend this month focusing on spirituality with your kids, encourage them to continue to say their prayer or practice meditation so that they will continue to live spiritually long after this month is over.

When any of you face obstacles, stop for a moment to consider whether you need to persevere on the path you are on, or if it's time to go in a different direction. Maybe you need to ask for divine intervention and then be open to help or guidance that comes your way. And when you or someone in your family is feeling overwhelmed and disconnected from God or your higher power, try to look a little deeper to see the sacred presence at work in your lives. It may not always be obvious, or easy to find, but I believe it's there.

Month Twelve

A SENSE OF PURPOSE

Following your life's path with passion, and a map!

On top of everything else you do as a parent, now you need to give your kids a sense of purpose? Well, yes. If you instill all these wonderful values in your kids and let them loose in the world, where exactly are they headed? You don't want to set them off on a path so narrow that they don't truly experience the journey. On the other hand, you don't want them to wander aimlessly, not really having a sense of why they are here at all. Of course, it's not your job to plan your children's life journeys and pack their socks and underwear. After all, we're talking about their journeys. But it's your responsibility to give them a sense of direction. That's what this month is all about.

Equipped with the values they've learned throughout this year, they will be well on their way. Just do your best to point them in the right direction so they can find whatever path they are meant to follow. And then, let go, at least a little bit.

But what is a sense of purpose? Some people call it conviction. My husband calls it having a dream and following it with passion. The way I see it, having a dream for your life is like a road and passion is the unwavering sense of direction that keeps you moving forward despite obstacles thrown in your path. Together, that's a sense of purpose. If you're like most parents, you want your children to have dreams *and* a roadmap of sorts so those dreams can actually be realized.

After all, in my experience, and I'd bet in yours as well, dreams don't typically just come true with no effort. Usually, dreams come true because the dreamer helps make it happen by focusing on and working toward the dream, and by staying the course even when it seems impossible.

For instance, let's say your ten-year-old son has a really warm and outgoing personality and loves to cook. He has always been open to trying new foods and new experiences, and even comes up with his own recipes. Or your eight-year-old daughter has a quiet, introspective, and kind personality. She is always playing with every building toy she can get her hands on and loves to draw and paint. Those qualities and interests can help your children start to see what direction they might be starting to take in their lives, and it can even help them find career paths when they are ready.

But having a sense of purpose is not just about having direction in terms of career goals. Sure, what a person does for a living can be an important part of it, but it's not the whole picture. And certainly many people don't have the luxury of following in a particular career path for financial or other reasons. In that case, does that mean that child will not have a sense of purpose in his or her life? Of course not. Whatever paths we take in our lives, if we are living our values, we are never far off course.

Anyway, career success isn't always what it seems. Two people who follow identical career paths in terms of the jobs they do can have completely different ideas about what their sense of purpose is. To help your children understand the distinction, tell them a story about two business people who own their own small companies. The first person might follow business practices that carefully consider the environment and are respectful to her employees, as well as committing to give back a percentage of profits to the community. Clearly, that person's sense of purpose is centered on an awareness and respect for people beyond herself. The second business owner may be interested in profit to the detriment of the environment, her employees, and maybe even to her own family. Both people may even become wealthy through their businesses. These two may look like they are traveling the same path, but in truth they are on two completely different journeys.

So, although this month is about helping your kids start to think about what they really want to be when they grow up, it's also about inspiring them to think about *why* they want to follow that particular path. And since you have taught them lessons about commitment, respect for others, and compassion, as well as all the values you've focused on in the past year, they can also draw on those as they follow their own paths in life.

Supplies Needed for This Month's Exercises:

- Thirty 3-inch by 5-inch or 4-inch by 6-inch index cards per child, in colors other than white if possible. Younger children tend to prefer the bigger cards as it gives them plenty of room to write.
- You'll also need some yarn and a poster board for each child. Please note—the yarn is used to make a type of necklace worn by the child when they are doing the weekly exercise. If you have younger children in your family, for safety purposes, I would suggest using a wooden ice-cream stick, tape, and a small piece of card stock or construction paper instead of making a necklace.
- You'll be using a large poster board for each child for the one-time exercise, along with markers or crayons in various colors.

Daily Exercise: Getting to Know Me

This exercise can give you a glimpse into your children's thoughts that you might not otherwise have had. But the main point of the exercise is to help children get to know themselves a little better. For instance, a child may already know that she loves music, but has she really given any thought about what that might mean in her life? Does she want to take guitar lessons, listen to music all the time, or be a professional musician some day? Or none of the above?

To help figure out what direction a child might want to take in his or her life, every day this month, ask your kids to take an index card and write down something they know about themselves. Give them guidelines each day by asking questions like, "What is something so important to you that you have to do it every day?" In my house, my son might answer, "I can't go a day without reading a book." Or, ask your kids to name three things they love. My daughter's answer might be, "I love animals, gymnastics, and sweets." I encourage parents to participate as well. You may feel like you already have a strong sense of who you are. Even so, you may learn things about yourself, and your kids will certainly enjoy hearing your answers to the daily questions and getting to know you better.

Keep the index cards in those handy index card boxes found at most office supply stores or just hold them together with a rubber band or a ribbon. If your kids are very visual and love color like mine do, you might consider getting each child a specific color index card for the month. That's what we do in our family. It also helps to prevent the cards getting mixed up, because you will be referring to them for the one-time exercise at the end of the month.

Examples of Questions for the "Getting to Know Me" Daily Exercise:

- If you won an Olympic gold medal would you want it to be for an individual or team sport, and what sport would it be?
- If you had a whole afternoon to do anything you wanted, what would it be?
- Imagine you are writing your autobiography . . . what's the title?
- When you grow up, would you like to get married and have children? If so, how many?

- Imagine I handed you a picture and it made you smile from ear to ear. What are you seeing in the picture?
- What academic subject (not counting recess or gym class) do you look forward to at school and why?
- If you could go on only one of these trips with your family what would you choose—going on a safari in Africa, helping to build houses for Habitat for Humanity in New Orleans, swimming and snorkeling in Hawaii, or visiting ancient ruins and museums in Greece? Why?
- Imagine there is a contest where you win first prize . . . what is the contest about and what prize would you win?
- Is a science project at school more fun if you do it in a group or by yourself?
- What is your biggest dream for your life?
- Would you rather spend an afternoon watching a funny movie or doing a hands-on activity like making pottery, making a cake from scratch, or building something?
- Would cuddling with a pet make you feel better if you were sad? If so, what kind of pet would it be?
- If you had to get up in front of your class, would you rather recite a poem, sing a song, play an instrument, or do a dance?
- If someone wanted to honor you by naming something after you, what would that thing be and why?
- Write down something we don't already know about you.
- If you were an instrument in the orchestra, what instrument would you be and why?
- When people get to know you, what three words would they use to describe you?
- What three words would you use to describe yourself?

- If you could spend the day shadowing a grownup at their job, what job would it be and why?
- If you were the voice for an animated animal in a movie, what animal would you want to play?
- If a magician was on stage and asked for a volunteer from the audience, would you raise your hand? Why or why not?
- Do you prefer to live in a climate that is mostly warm and sunny all year long, or one in which the seasons change?
- If your class at school decided to make a movie and you had first choice about what you would do in the project, would you choose to write the script, design the set, act, direct, or sell tickets?
- Imagine that you are grown up and working in a profession you love. What would you usually be wearing to work?
- If you could be really good at something you're not actually good at now, what would it be?
- What color describes your personality the best and why?
- If you have a big project at school, are you more likely to finish it on time if you handle it all on your own, or if someone regularly reminds you to stay on track?
- Where do you want to live when you grow up—a city, small town, in the country, or traveling from place to place without really having a home base?
- Do you consider yourself a follower or a leader? Why?
- Which is more fun—to make something with your own hands or to think up an idea with your mind?
- What country would you like to visit and why?
- When you grow up, will the work you do inspire people, help them, or make them happy?
- If you invented something today, what would it be?

Each day as they write down their answers, you and your spouse or partner will start to have a better sense of what really matters to your children. Many of these questions require that kids look ahead and imagine their lives as grownups in a fairly practical way. This may be the first time most kids have done this other than talking in faraway generalities about what they want to be when they grow up. As you go through the month, these questions will hopefully help your children have a clearer picture of what is truly important to them and will act as a compass, leading them in the direction of their dreams.

Parents Shari and Gary experienced this month with their two daughters, ages eight and nine. When they asked their younger daughter what color best describes her personality, she chose yellow because "I'm bright and I like to chat with people. It's a happy color!" Their older daughter was asked whom she would like to shadow at a job. One of the professions she chose was environmentalist, because as she put it, "When you do something for the world, it makes you feel good." When asked what she would do if she had the whole day to herself, she responded that after a breakfast at her favorite bagel place, she would spend her day volunteering. These answers prompted Shari to try to work more opportunities for volunteering into their family schedule.

Variations on Getting to Know Me:

Some children may be intimidated by answering personal questions about themselves, even if it is just for their parents. Another way to do this would be to give them multiple-choice questions on an index card each day, like "What word best describes you . . . serious, friendly, or athletic?" Then they could just circle the answer they feel represents them the best. Some kids would enjoy suggesting questions themselves.

Other children might feel more comfortable drawing pictures to express themselves, so the questions could be structured more like requests. For example, "Imagine you are a grownup and happily working in your profession. Draw a picture of where you spend your work days."

Another idea would be to let your children write little books about themselves, with a new entry every day. If they are a little self-conscious, you might encourage them to create a fictional character with the same name as they have, and each day write down something about that character on a new page—what he or she loves to do, is good at, and what brings the character the most joy. You can use the questions provided as a springboard for what moves the story along each day.

Weekly Exercise: Taking Initiative

The tricky thing about following your dreams is that ultimately, no one else can make them come true but you. You have to take charge of your dreams and follow them with determination and passion if they are going to have a chance at really happening. It takes initiative to make dreams come true. If you want your dreams to come true, do something about it!

In order to inspire initiative in your kids, do this exercise designed to encourage them to cultivate this valuable quality once a week during Sense of Purpose Month.

Have your kids make a necklace out of cardboard and yarn, writing the word "Initiative" on the cardboard. There should be only one necklace that will be shared by the whole family. Once a week during this month, each child gets a turn to wear the necklace and therefore "take" the initiative on what will happen that night. In my house, my daughter might choose to have an art show with all the photographs she has taken in recent weeks. She would be in charge of coming up with the idea and organizing the whole event. My son might decide to make a film about the family. It's up to your child to decide what to do, and you should let him or her be in charge of all the details and planning.

This exercise builds on the self-respect you have explored earlier in the year. It also helps your kids foster a sense of confidence and pride in their own capabilities. Doing this exercise may not be easy for those of us who plan much of our children's lives. But letting someone else take initiative and responsibility for something can actually be quite a relief to a busy parent. Who knew?

Be sure that it's clear when your kids take initiative in this exercise that it doesn't mean they are running the house. It means they get to take charge of a certain thing and truly be in charge of whatever it is. Let's say your six-year-old son would love to make lunch for the family. That means he has to set the table and prepare the food (avoiding the stove, of course). Maybe he makes PB & J sandwiches for lunch. He would also be responsible for clearing away the plates and if he's not old enough to wash the dishes by hand, he could load the dishwasher, or just stack the plates on the counter. The point is he would be in charge of the meal.

Or maybe your ten-year-old daughter wants to plan "Family Night" and you always have pizza. She can call and order the pizza, but you may have to pay—though in our house we keep a jar with money for family night meals, so you might consider doing that to have some cash on hand. Or if your daughter has money, she can pay. Then she could also choose the movie or board game that the family will play. She would set up the game or put in the movie and be in charge of the evening.

Parents have two options for participation in this exercise. You can take turns with your kids in taking initiative and plan an event for the whole family. Or since that's probably what you do all the time, you can also participate in this exercise by *not* taking initiative. In other words, if your son is getting peanut butter and jelly all over the kitchen counter, don't step in to fix it! Let him handle it. That in itself is a good exercise for parents. Sometimes we need to let our kids impress us with what they can do rather than insert ourselves into the situation to do it our way.

By the way, if you have a large family, in order to give everyone a chance to take initiative, you may decide to have different family members be in charge of different things throughout a weekend, for example. As always, do what works best for your particular family.

Variations on Taking Initiative:

If this kind of exercise isn't a good fit for your child—for instance, they have difficulty making decisions—you might try to ease into it. Instead of having them "take initiative" for a whole evening for example, you could simply pass the necklace from one family member to another for a short while. That way each person could take charge for one decision at a time. In terms of a "Family Night" for example, that might mean your son chooses what to order or make for dinner. That part of the night is up to him. Then he passes the necklace to his big brother, who then decides what game to play or movie to watch. The grown-ups should play a part too, especially if that makes your kids feel more comfortable with this exercise.

Again, a necklace made with yarn could be a safety issue for little children. So even if the children doing the exercise are older, if there are any young children in the house, I would suggest using a piece of card stock paper with the word "Initiative" on it, and simply tape or glue it to a clean ice-cream stick. Or make an "Initiative Badge" with construction paper and tape it to the shirt of whomever is in charge at that time.

One-Time Exercise: Life Map on a Mission

At the end of the month, your kids will no doubt have learned a few things about themselves, so it is time to move on to the one-time exercise for Sense of Purpose Month. For this exercise, get out a large poster board and have each child make a map of where he or she would like to go in their lives, almost as if it's a physical destination. After all, life doesn't come with a GPS system! Start by having them draw a little picture of themselves on a piece of construction paper, cutting it out and putting tape on the back. This way they can attach it to the map they'll make and they can move these mini versions of themselves along as they meet their goals.

Then talk about some of the answers they gave to the questions in the daily exercise. You may start to see patterns in your children's answers. We did. It turns out Grace consistently chose to be outdoors whenever that option came up in a question, and that she typically preferred being with people to being alone. We talked about some of the things she might want to experience and accomplish in her life. Since she loves animals, gymnastics, and sweets, how does she see those things being a part of her life as she grows up? Does she see them as childhood things that she will grow out of or as things that will always bring her joy? In my daughter's case, she feels that her love of animals is so important to her that she wants to be a veterinarian and have pets like a cat and dog. She plans to continue with gymnastics for the near future, and as for sweets—chocolate will always be part of her life. Who can blame her?

As you talk about your children's answers to the daily questions, ask them to create some goals they can have for their lives. To use the example of my daughter, she could write one of those big goals like becoming a veterinarian on the poster board. Then, she would tape the mini version of herself on the map and put it fairly far away from her goal of becoming an animal doctor because at age seven, she has a long way to go to get there. That can seem intimidating to a child, so as you discuss larger goals, you can talk to your children about what smaller steps they might need to take in order to get to that particular goal in their lives. Explain that just like a geographical map, there will be a journey to get to their destination. It isn't going to be instant and most likely it won't be easy.

Encourage your children to see that as a good thing. Let them know that none of this is written in stone and along the way they may find other interests and dreams they want to pursue. As long as the new paths they create for themselves are consistent with their values, they'll still be on the right track for themselves as individuals.

As my daughter is creating her Life Map, my son is making his as well. Of course, his map looks different because he has different dreams than his sister does. He is passionate about acting, and making movies. He wants to create films that make people happy. At this point, we have both kids put dots representing things that may help them get to their destinations. These dots look similar to how small towns look on a geographical map, but instead of the name of a physical destination like a town, the kids write down what the dots represent to them. One dot on their journey might be getting a college education while another refers to learning to speak a foreign language. They are individual goals that ideally will help them achieve their biggest dreams. I also encourage my kids to put things on their maps that they can achieve in the near future, like finishing second grade or getting to the next level in karate. This way they can start to move those mini versions of themselves along on their map and start to see real progress.

This is a good time to talk with your children about the values they have learned on this yearlong journey you have taken as a family. Having a sense of purpose in life is not just about getting from point A to point B. Even more important than the journey itself is what kind of person is taking the journey. Are they grateful? Are they compassionate? Are they joyful? Teach your children that values are what bring meaning to their journeys. They are the guideposts that help keep them going in the right direction.

For instance, if we think about my daughter's goal of being a veterinarian or my son's goal of being a filmmaker, does it matter how they get there as long as they achieve their goals? You better believe it does. Just like in the instance I mentioned earlier about two business people who appeared to have achieved the same thing, our children have choices to make that can impact their life journeys. They can cheat on tests, push fellow students around to keep the choice opportunities for themselves, and step on anyone who gets in their way. Or they can be grateful for the opportunities they have, respect themselves and others, and live their lives with integrity and compassion, forgiving themselves and others for missteps. They can commit to working hard in veterinary or film school, and when times get tough, they can rely on their inner strength and spirituality to get them through. A love of learning and a cheerful attitude can keep life interesting and joyful. They are not going on their journeys alone. Their values go with them every step of the way. Ask your children to find a way to illustrate on their life maps how their values will be a part of their journeys. It might be represented as a vehicle like a car or boat that helps them get where they are going or something they wear or carry with them like luggage.

To go a little deeper with this exercise, your children should write their own personal motto or mission statement. You can help your children figure out their motto by looking over their life map and encouraging them to incorporate their goals and values. If your child is like the little boy I described earlier who loves people, adventure, and cooking, his personal motto might be "To cook delicious food around the world and always have friends and family to share it with." Or if your daughter is like the quiet, kind little girl who likes to build and create things, her motto might be "I will build pretty houses for people to live in and will help poor people with the money I earn." Just like the Life Map itself, these mottos may change over time. But just having this personal motto can start to empower children to believe that their dreams are within reach.

Keep this Life Map with the personal motto in each child's bedroom long after this month is over so your children can look at it, add to it, and move themselves along on their journey.

Variations on Life Map on a Mission:

Your children might prefer to get some building toys and build a topographical-style map complete with obstacles and markers representing goals and ways to achieve them. They might prefer taking an existing map (with your permission) and using colorful markers to map out their own life journey. You and your kids might enjoy making a map together on the computer. The idea of the exercise is to encourage children to explore what is important to them—what they love, what their dreams are—and to help them see that achieving a big goal often involves accomplishing smaller goals along the way.

The key is to do this exercise in a way that will be fun and memorable for your children.

Staying Power

Since focusing a month on having a sense of purpose, my children each identify more strongly with their dreams of being a veterinarian and a filmmaker. My daughter has honored her commitment to take care of her kitten, Riley, and shows a lot of promise as a vet. And my son is already working on his own scripts and is considering taking a film class. But the best part is that they also have started seeing themselves as people who are grateful and kind and honest on their journeys. Our values have started to become their values.

After this month is over, as you see your children accomplish their smaller goals, congratulate them and remind them to move their "mini-selves" along on their life maps. Let them know they are getting one step closer to accomplishing their dreams. Give them many opportunities to take initiative and to show you how smart, creative, and inventive they can be when they're in charge.

And remember, this month, like the whole year of values, is not only meant to be for your children. It's for the grownups too. I know I should say "adults" but you know how it is, your whole vocabulary changes when you become a parent. It's as if we morph into completely different beings when we have children. But our dreams are still in there somewhere. So if you are one of those moms or dads who have lost sight of your dreams, use this month as a starting point to find them again. Do the exercises, answer the questions, make the Life Map, and find your path. Your values will guide you, just as they'll guide your children.

And if you are already right where you want to be, show your children how you got there. Share your journey with them and let them know how your values, the very ones you have been sharing with them, helped you find your own sense of purpose.

conclusion

You know how when you're hanging out with one of your friends and you stay for one more cup of coffee? This chapter is kind of like that. This is the part of the book where we kind of sit down together at the kitchen table, so to speak, and talk about where you go from here.

First of all, there are two ways to approach this last chapter. If you've read the whole book and are now ready to embark on this yearlong journey of values with your children, that's terrific. You have a great overview of how the year is planned out in terms of the exercises. And you have a good sense that this will not eat up all your spare time—like you have any in the first place! Most days, the exercises will take about five minutes. Of course, you will have conversations about each value throughout each of the twelve months. But I'm sure you already talk to your kids about values— this system just helps you focus on one value at a time. That's really the whole point of this book. You are doing something you want to do anyway—teaching your values to your kids. Through this month-by-month approach, you can do that more intentionally, efficiently, and effectively in a way that will last.

If you are reading this chapter after you have completed this journey with your families, you may be wondering, "What next? Are we done?" Well, that all depends. Do you feel you and your family got enough out of it? Maybe you have some momentum now and would like to give it another go round, and build on what you've accomplished so far. You may be able to find even deeper lessons the second time around. By all means, do this as many times as you like. Or just repeat the values your kids need more help with. It's very personalized—each family will ultimately do it in their own way. To keep it fresh, if you used the original exercises the first time around, try one of the variations I've provided for each exercise. Now that you're experienced with this system, you and your kids may want to come up with your own variations. Or change the order of the values. Ask your kids what values they want to focus on. Change it up to keep it interesting to you and your children. Personally, we've done it for almost three years now and that has been great for our family. That's because, as my kids grow up a little more each year, they are able to understand the value that much better. Believe it or not, they still look forward to it. They still get something out of focusing a month on each value.

So if you haven't begun this year with your family yet, I encourage you to get started. You can do it! If you've already done a year of values, keep going in whatever direction works for your family. As parents, we have tremendous power to shape the future by making sure we do everything we can to give our children our values—deeply felt beliefs that will shape their lives, guide their journey, and as Thoreau said "turn the world around."

acknowledgments

First of all, I must express my deepest gratitude to God for opening doors in my life and for giving me the courage to walk through them.

When I first came up with this system of teaching values to my children, I didn't see it as a book. It was merely something I did with my husband to teach our kids our values. It is a book now because three people saw in this idea much more than I ever imagined.

My sister Clare O'Donohue, a talented and successful mystery writer, was the first one who heard about what my husband and I were doing to impart our values to our kids and said, "That's a book." I tried to tell her, no, it's just something we do with our family, but she would have none of that. I am profoundly grateful to Clare for her encouragement, advice, and support throughout every step of this process. Not to mention that she brought the idea to her agent, Sharon Bowers, who also said, "That's a book." Sharon encouraged me to write a proposal and became my agent as well. I deeply appreciate Sharon's faith in this idea, her tenacity in helping me polish the proposal, and her expertise at choosing the right publishers to consider it. The third person who made this book possible is Chelsea King at Adams Media, who believed in the proposal enough to become my first editor. I am so thankful for Chelsea's faith in this idea and for everything she has done on my behalf. I am humbled that she and Adams Media would give me this opportunity. I am also extremely grateful to my second editor, Meredith O'Hayre, for her guidance and patience with a first-time author, and for her graciousness. Her input and creativity made the book better in every way. Sincere thanks to Frank Rivera for his fresh and creative cover design and for instinctively using my favorite color combination. I'm very grateful to interior book designer Michelle Kelly for her impeccable sense of style and attention to detail, both of which brought my words to life. Thank you also to copy editor Melanie Zimmerman for her meticulous work and diligence. I deeply appreciate everyone at Adams Media who contributed their creativity and talents to this project.

The wonderful parents who joined me with their children in this journey of teaching values generously gave their time, dedication, insights, suggestions, and support. I am forever grateful to Kate and Jeff, Nora and Eli, Happi and Jerry, Cara and Mark, Karen and Bill, Beth, Karen and Jeff, Lori and Kevin, Amy, Katie, Laurie and Jesse, and Shari and Gary for "family-testing" the exercises, for sharing their personal experiences, and for all the exceptional feedback they gave me. A special thank you to all the children who kid-tested the exercises—what can I say? You are all wonderful! I am very grateful to each and every one of you for your stories and for trying this system.

When my friends ask me with incredulity how in the world I found the time to write this book while working full-time and raising two children, I tell them in three words—my wonderful husband. For six months Jim cooked every meal, did mountains of laundry, packed school lunches, made the beds, and made sure I had the space and uninterrupted (well, usually) time to write. All this while he also worked full-time. I really can't express my gratitude enough to my husband. Without Jim's love and support, I wouldn't have been able to write a single chapter. And although I missed my children terribly throughout this process and they missed me right back, they found ways to make it easier on me. Lovely Gracie's "warm hugs" always were just what I needed. And the hot cups of my favorite green tea sweet Connor brought me sustained me as I wrote this book. My children are the reason for this system of teaching values, for this book, for everything in my life, and I love them indescribably.

I deeply appreciate my mother for giving me her values and fostering them in me even in my adulthood, and for her prayers, confidence, and the countless hours of babysitting, not to mention her excellent copy editing—I love you dearly and I am more grateful than I can say. To my father who started a long ago conversation with me about values that has stayed with me my whole life—I love you and miss you, Dad, and I still remember the lessons you taught me.

Thanks to my entire extended family for all the love and support, especially Mary Jo and George.

Much gratitude to Margaret Smith, Peggy McIntyre, and Peggy Schroeder, who each gave of their time and helped me with this project. Thank you also to my wonderful colleagues, the "Short Turnarounds," Judy, McLane, Mike, Eric, Jay, Brian, Beth, Rachel, Joe, and Gia, with a special thanks to Sari and Yvette for their encouragement and friendship. And much appreciation to Ashlee Gillen and Gabriella Martinez for their assistance.

I am very grateful to Helen Scott, Certified Montessori teacher, for enlightening me about natural consequences and for her endless compassion and kindness. I am also thankful to my friend Bea Cunningham for her encouragement and to Jill for her creativity and insights. A special debt of gratitude to Michael, who has inspired me to be a better person and a better paren, and has always been there for me.

Lastly, to my dear friend George Washington, who shared a name with a president, but was in all other ways unique and irreplaceable. If it weren't for George, I would never have believed myself capable of embarking on this project. I made him a promise a few days after he died that the next time something came along in my life that I knew with certainty I could not do, I would do it for him. George, I kept my promise.

INDEX

about the author

Mary O'Donohue and her husband Jim have been married for fifteen years and have two children, Connor and Grace. She balances being a mom with a long career in television production. Mary has worked for ABC, CBS, and NBC network stations, on shows such as *Today* and *Meet the Press*, as well as on numerous music and entertainment programs including *MTV Unplugged, Mariah Carey at St. John the Divine Cathedral,* and *An Opryland Christmas*; and on many talk shows including *The Oprah Winfrey Show*. She's an avid traveler, having spent time in Ireland, England, Wales, France, Germany, Italy, Mexico, and China. She loves to read and has a passion for photography. Mary plans to donate at least 10 percent of her author's net profits to charities benefitting families and education. She can be reached through her website at *www.maryodonohue.com.*

about the foreword writer

Nancy Lilienthal, Ms Ed is the director of 43rd Street Kids Pre-school and has been an educator for the last thirty-seven years. She was part of the first wave of educators from the United States to discover, study, and adapt lessons from these now extremely popular schools, which promote strong parent involvement and a creative and integrated curriculum. In today's busy and stressed school environment, Nancy focuses on and promotes positive relationships between children, their parents, fellow students, and the world in which they live.